THE PRIMARY SUBJECT MANAGER'S HANDBOOKS SERIES

Management skills for SEN
coordinators in the primary school

THE SUBJECT LEADER'S HANDBOOKS

Series Editor: Mike Harrison, Centre for Primary Education, School of Education, The University of Manchester, Oxford Road, Manchester, M13 9DP

Coordinating mathematics across the primary school
Tony Brown

Coordinating English at Key Stage 1
Mick Waters and Tony Martin

Coordinating English at Key Stage 2
Mick Waters and Tony Martin

Coordinating science across the primary school
Lynn D. Newton and Douglas P. Newton

Coordinating information and communications technology across the primary school
Mike Harrison

Coordinating art across the primary school
Judith Piotrowski, Robert Clements and Ivy Roberts

Coordinating design and technology across the primary school
Alan Cross

Coordinating geography across the primary school
John Halocha

Coordinating history across the primary school
Julie Davies and Jason Redmond

Coordinating music across the primary school
Sarah Hennessy

Coordinating religious education across the primary school
Derek Bastide

Coordinating physical education across the primary school
Carole Raymond

Management skills for SEN coordinators in the primary school
Sylvia Phillips, Jennifer Goodwin and Rosita Heron

Building a whole school assessment policy
Mike Wintle and Mike Harrison

The primary coordinator and OFSTED re-inspection
Phil Gadsby and Mike Harrison

Coordinating the curriculum in the smaller primary school
Mick Waters

· FALMER PRESS · Taylor & Francis Group

Management skills for SEN coordinators in the primary school

Sylvia Phillips, Jennifer Goodwin and Rosita Heron

UK   Falmer Press, 1 Gunpowder Square, London, EC4A 3DE

USA   Falmer Press, Taylor & Francis Inc., 325 Chestnut Street, 8th Floor, Philadelphia, PA 19106

First published in 1999

A catalogue record for this book is available from the British Library

ISBN 0 7507 0697 x paper

Library of Congress Cataloging-in-Publication Data are available on request

Jacket design by Carla Turchini

Typeset in 10/14pt Melior and printed by Graphicraft Limited, Hong Kong

Contents

Part two
Managing teaching and learning

Part three
Working with others

Part four
Resources

List of figures

Series editor's preface

This book has been prepared for primary teachers charged with the responsibility of acting as the special needs coordinator (SENCO) for their schools. It has been written particularly for those who are new (or relatively new) to the role and indeed new to the responsibilities of management within a school structure. It forms part of a series of new publications that set out to advise such teachers on the complex issues of improving teaching and learning through managing elements and aspects of the primary school curriculum.

Nothing should take teachers away from their most important role, of serving the best interests of the class of children in their care and this book and others in the series does not wish to diminish that mission. However, the increasing complexity of the primary curriculum and society's expanding expectations, make it very difficult for individual class teachers to keep up to date with every development. Within traditional subject areas there has been an explosion of knowledge and as in new fields introduced such as science, technology, design, problem solving and health education, not to mention the uses of computers. These are now considered entitlements for all primary children. Furthermore, we now expect all children to succeed at these studies, not just the fortunate few. All this has overwhelmed a class teacher system largely unchanged since the inception of primary schools.

Primary class teachers cannot therefore possibly be an expert in every aspect of the curriculum they are required to teach nor to provide for all their pupils without help. To whom can they turn for help? It is unrealistic to assume that such support will be available from the headteacher whose responsibilities have grown ever wider since the 1988 Education Reform Act. Constraints, including additional staff costs, and the loss of benefits from the strength and security of the class teacher system, militate against wholesale adoption of specialist or semi-specialist teaching. Help, therefore, has to come from exploiting the talents of teachers themselves, in a process of mutual support. Hence primary schools have chosen many and varied systems of consultancy or subject coordination which best suit the needs of their children and the current expertise of the staff. The institution of the SENCO formally recognises the need for a teacher to promote the interests of pupils who, at some time in their school careers need particular support and recognises that primary teachers may need some guidance on how to provide it.

There are many good publications available for SENCOs, and it may be worth asking why there is a need for another. There are three main answers to this question. Firstly, this book does not, as do many of the other handbooks, offer a *guide* to the Code of Practice (DFE, 1994) and how to *interpret* the Code. There is an assumption that readers have a greater familiarity with the Code than in earlier publications. Secondly, this is the only book to date which is explicitly written for primary school coordinators, who have to carry out their role, often in addition to their responsibilities as a full-time class teacher. Finally Sylvia Phillips, Rosita Heron, and Jennifer Goodwin, as do other authors in the series, emphasise the significance of management and coordination skills rather than just knowledge and understanding, in this case understanding of children with special educational needs. As such the book should be useful to support the independent study and professional development of a new SENCO and be an appropriate text for a SENCO (or intending SENCO) attending a formal course of SENCO training. This book also offers practical guidance and many insights for anyone in the school who has a responsibility for ensuring that all pupils have access to the curriculum including teachers with an overall role in coordinating the whole or key stage curriculum and the deputy head and headteacher. It will also be of interest to the SEN nominated governor.

Fundamental to the book is that a SENCO has to *coordinate* provision on a scale which few other primary teachers share. The SENCO has to learn to work through others. Currently, as the authors point out in the first chapter, no other primary coordinator has a role which is specified in a government publication, with an explicit set of expectations. Whilst some of the skills and attributes associated with being a SENCO may 'come naturally' it is possible to develop and learn many of them and Sylvia Phillips, Rosita Heron, and Jennifer Goodwin suggest how.

The book sets out these fundamental values and personal qualities which a successful SENCO will need:
- a *vision* of inclusive education and an understanding of how all pupils needs can be met in a mainstream school;
- a strong personal belief (firmly backed by skills and knowledge) that *all* children can be helped to learn successfully and therefore raise their levels of achievement;
- an ability to empathise with children, teachers, parents and other adults;
- a willingness to be an advocate for children with SEN (even if this may not, at first, be popular with colleagues);
- an ability to be a sympathetic and active learner;
- an openness and preparedness to share professional skills with others;
- an ability to think, plan and work flexibly;
- patience, tolerance and enthusiasm;
- enthusiasm and a capacity for positive thinking without appearing over-zealous, over-bearing or evangelical (and thereby alienating colleagues);
- sincerity in their interactions with others.

Above all, a SENCO must be a good teacher who is prepared to examine his or her own teaching and offer leadership to her colleagues.

Leadership functions in primary schools have increasingly been shared with class teachers through the policy of coordination for the past twenty years, especially to improve the consistency of work in language and mathematics. Since then each school has developed their own system and the series recognises some of the possible tensions of holding a dual role.

This series sets out to help teachers to achieve the coordination aspect of this role. The books each deal with specific issues whilst at the same time providing an overview of general themes in the management of the subject curriculum. The purpose of the series is to give practical guidance and support to teachers, in particular, what to do and how to do it. They each offer help on the production, development and review of policies and schemes of work; the organisation of resources; and developing strategies for improving the management of the curriculum and its implementation.

Within this book the authors address you, the SENCO, directly, in a 'reader-friendly' style, and hope to give you the opportunity to develop many of the above skills and qualities, in addition (or as part of) those described more fully in the National Standards. It is essentially a practical book, including examples of materials and containing some activities developed to engage you in reflecting on your practices and ideas, and help you to become more confident in your ability to discharge the responsibilities required by the SENCO role.

In making decisions about which aspects of knowledge and skills to explore in the book the authors have been guided by:
- the Code of Practice (DFE, 1994) which they demonstrate has raised the status and profile of SENCOs in ways which can only help to improve achievements for all pupils;
- the National Standards for SENCOs (TTA, 1998);
- and their experiences in training a great many SENCOs who continue to work with them, maintaining their credibility and helping them to keep their feet on the ground.

Thus the book's authors are able to offer many practical hints and useful advice in order that you can establish and maintain a high quality provision for children with a range of needs as an important part of the school's curriculum. The book will help those attempting to develop a whole-school view of the progress all children can make and in the various ways they learn. The authors draw on their considerable experience as teacher educators. Together they have put together a most readable book which will help SENCOs develop both the expertise they will need and the managerial perspective necessary to enthuse and inform others.

The Green Paper (DfEE, 1998) sets out the present government's aims for achievement for children with special educational needs by the year 2002. We hope that this book goes some way to helping SENCOs play their part in achieving the 'Excellence for *All* Children' promised in the title of that paper.

Mike Harrison, Series Editor
July 1998

Acknowledgments

The authors and Publisher would like to thank the following for permission to reproduce:

Verbal Skills for Managers — Adapted from *Effective Change: Twenty Ways to Make it Happen* by Leigh (1988) and is reproduced with the permission of the author and the publishers, the Institute of Personnel and Development, IPD House, 35 Camp Road, London SW19 4UX.

The Three Circles Model from *Effective Leadership* by Adair (1983). Permission granted by Macmillan.

The Agenda Bell — Tropman (1996) *Effective Meetings; Improving group decision making* pp30. Copyright © 1996 by Sage Publications Ltd. Reprinted by Permission of Sage Publications, Inc.

Characteristics of ineffective and effective meetings — This table is adapted from *Improve your people skills* by Honey (1988) and is reproduced with the permission of the author and the publishers, the Institute of Personnel and Development, IPD House, 35 Camp Road, London SW19 4UX.

Reviewing the school's policy for SEN; Example of an IEP; SEN professional development questionnaire — Phillips, Cockett and Louvre (1996) *Special Educational Needs: Putting the Code to Work* pp15–17 and pp95. Permission granted by the publishers Financial Times Management.

DfE (1994) *Code of Practice on the Identification and Assessment of Special Educational Needs* para 2.14 and 2.93. Crown Copyright is reproduced with the permission of the Controller of Her Majesty's Stationery Office.

Self-rating inventory adapted from Everard and Morris (1996) *Effective School Management* pp98–99. Reprinted by permission of Paul Chapman and Sage Publications Ltd.

Part one

The SEN coordinator as manager: Developing management skills

Chapter 1

The role and responsibilities of a SEN coordinator

Introduction

The role of SEN coordinator is unique in that it is the only coordinator role which has its responsibilities defined within a government publication. Not only that, but all mainstream schools are expected to have such a designated teacher. Your starting point then, in developing your role, should be to consider the responsibilities identified in the *Code of Practice on the Identification and Assessment of Special Educational Needs* (DFE, 1994a), paragraph 2:14.

The SENCO has responsibility for:

- the day-to-day operation of the school's SEN policy
- liaising with and advising fellow teachers
- co-ordinating provision for children with special educational needs
- maintaining the school's SEN register and overseeing the records on all pupils with special educational needs
- liaising with parents of children with special educational needs
- contributing to the in-service training of staff
- liaising with external agencies including the Educational Psychology Service and other support agencies, medical and social services and voluntary bodies

(DFE, 1994a, pp. 9–10)

Whilst the existence of this list of responsibilities is useful — it provides you with support for your work with colleagues and helps you to negotiate your more precise role within the school's management structure — it is not overly prescriptive. You can still show initiative in how you meet these responsibilities.

If you are just taking up the role, these responsibilities can seem daunting, particularly as, in primary schools, they are usually in addition to full-time teaching. Indeed, the Code of Practice recognised the magnitude of the role, suggesting that governors and headteachers:

❝ . . . *may need to give careful thought to the SEN Co-ordinator's timetable in the light of this Code and in the context of resources available to the school.*　　(DFE, 1994a, p. 10)

A recent survey on the implementation of the Code of Practice (Lewis, 1996) found that most SENCOs welcomed both the Code and their role, although they cited some obstacles to discharging their responsibilities (particularly resources, time and status). For primary SENCOs the predominant problem was that the position had to be added to 'a portfolio of responsibilities already undertaken by the class teacher (or deputy headteacher)' (Lewis, 1996).

Negotiating some 'time release' to undertake key aspects of your role might be one of the major tasks ahead of you. However, if you are to do so, you must be able to make a strong case based on an understanding of your role in the context of your school. A plaintive cry for 'more time' is unlikely to be heeded. If you have considered the nature of your role, how you are to carry out specific tasks and your management style, then you will be able to identify:

- **why** you need to have time without a class (i.e. what you will do in the time);
- **how** much time you need;
- **when** the time is needed;
- **whether** the time is needed on a short-term or long-term basis.

Until you have really examined your role and your own professional skills and development, you cannot (and should not) make hasty decisions about implementation.

Examples of these tasks may be:

■ *You wish to visit 1 or 2 schools to see their SEN provision.*
This is a short-term need for professional development. Visits could perhaps take place during one or two 'professional development days' (or half-day release from school, with/without 'cover').

■ *You need time to manage paperwork and meet parents/other professionals.*
This is a long-term need. Some SENCOs are excused from 'assembly' for this: in some schools the head has arranged for supply cover for a set time each week (varying from one hour to two days a week!) Some responsibilities are re-allocated to teachers *or* (as in the case of meeting parents) to the headteacher.

■ *You would like time to work collaboratively with other teachers in the classroom.*
This might be to support them in assessing needs or in modifying teaching materials or providing a 'model for teaching'. This may require short- or long-term 'cover' arrangements.

Although the Code of Practice may be amended in an attempt to reduce some of the bureaucracy and paperwork it has led to, the key responsibilities listed at the beginning of this chapter are unlikely to change. The TTA's National Standards for SENCOs (TTA, 1998) identify four key areas of SEN coordination in relation to the tasks involved and there is general acceptance of these main areas.

The TTA paper identifies four key areas of SEN coordination:

■ Strategic Direction and Development of SEN Provision in the School
■ Teaching and Learning
■ Leading and Managing Staff
■ Efficient and Effective Deployment of Staff and Resources

(TTA, 1998, p. 11)

In order to undertake the tasks involved, SENCOs will need knowledge and understanding and a set of skills and attributes. Some of these requirements would be identified as 'subject knowledge' in the case of a subject leader/coordinator, and can be interpreted as 'knowledge, understanding, skills and attributes related to SEN', whereas others relate more clearly to the role of coordinator — a middle manager/leadership role. It is clearly very important that as a SENCO you keep up to date with developments in the field of SEN (and education generally) and that you feel confident in your own teaching. This book is, however, more concerned with helping you to develop the management skills you will need as a SENCO.

Consideration of the TTA National Standards and a list of 'competencies' drawn up by the SEN Training Consortium (SENTC, 1996) at the request of the DFE (reproduced as Appendix A), has led us to identify the following management skills which form the basis of this book.

Management skills for SENCOs
- leading and managing teams
- managing people
- chairing meetings
- consultancy (advising, liaising)
- planning, maintaining, reviewing and evaluating systems and policies including preparing and managing inspections
- supporting people (colleagues, parents, pupils)
- administration (including managing paperwork and time)
- coordinating (provision and support)
- communication (spoken and written)
- monitoring, reviewing, evaluation of pupil's progress
- managing material resources and finance
- self-management
- planning/delivering professional development for self and others

There is a strong emphasis on good interpersonal skills.

If you are to be an effective coordinator, you must, therefore, begin by examining more closely the nature of the role and undertaking a personal audit of your professional development in relation to that role. We think there are four significant aspects to consider at this stage:
- the importance of whole school policies;
- role/job descriptions;
- personal/professional development;
- supportive school structures.

A whole school policy

Since the Education Act of 1981 was implemented (in 1983) there has been an emphasis on 'a whole school approach to SEN'. Whilst this requires someone to coordinate and manage the policy, processes and provision to meet children's SEN, an underlying principle is that most pupils' SEN will be identified, met and monitored by class teachers. Moss (1995) offers this advice:

> *a large part of your role involves trying to ensure that your colleagues do their part in assessing and making provision for all the children with special educational needs in your school.*
>
> (Moss, 1995, p. m1)

Many primary SENCOs are uncomfortable with this suggestion, feeling it implies a status they do not have. In addition, they may be reluctant to place what may appear to be 'further burdens' on colleagues already known to be feeling under pressure. Yet enabling other teachers to assume their responsibility for children with SEN is an important aspect of the SENCO's role. In beginning to work out your role as a primary SENCO, as a manager and coordinator, we suggest that while you are reading the next three sections in this chapter it is worthwhile:

- reflecting on the nature of your 'authority';
- considering how you might develop your own personal style of influence through your professional approach;
- exploring how you can persuade colleagues to work in partnership with you;
- considering who will support you by providing 'pressure' on others, should it ever be required.

A whole school approach helps you to define your role in relation to colleagues. It is as important for you to be as clear about *when* you will intervene directly with children as it is for your colleagues to realise their own responsibilities and know when they could be expected to meet SEN using their own resources. A first step towards this position is to have a clear, written description of your role.

Job/role description

It may well be that you already have a job description.
It is important to have a written statement agreed with the headteacher and governors which describes the scope (and limits) of your post. This can be written in a variety of ways, but it is usual to identify the:

■ key purpose(s) of the role (as in the Code of Practice);
■ key tasks involved;
■ line of responsibility (to whom are you accountable?).

In particular, the key tasks should show the extent to which you are directly involved in working with pupils and with colleagues. Very often teachers may seek assistance or help simply because they believe that they should do so, thinking that the knowledge, skills and sole responsibility for helping children with SEN resides within the SENCO. Your colleagues need to know when and under what circumstances you should be involved. Clarification of your role, to yourself, your headteacher and colleagues, governors and parents is important:

■ for a whole school policy to work;
■ for boosting the morale of all teachers by reinforcing their own professional skills and judgments in meeting SEN;
■ for you in managing your role as coordinator and managing and controlling your workload;
■ if you are to determine and plan for your own professional development.

A composite list of expectations of the tasks often required of SENCOs is presented at the end of this chapter. You might find it useful to check this against the tasks you have listed for in the suggested activity.

Personal professional development

It is important to undertake a personal audit of your professional strengths and experiences and to identify the areas where you need further development in order to discharge your responsibilities. We suggest that there are two main aspects to this:

Suggestion

Writing your job/role description

Title:

Purpose: Write a sentence to summarise the main purpose of your job.

Relationships/accountability: Where does your post lie in relation to the management structure? To whom are you accountable? How do you report to them? When?

Key tasks/responsibilities: List what it is you *do* (and under what circumstances).

1. Knowledge, skills, understandings and attributes which are essential to the 'subject' of SEN.
2. Knowledge, skills, understandings and attributes which are essential to the coordinating/managing role.

Of course there are areas where it is difficult to distinguish the two, but it is useful to recognise both aspects, particularly when undertaking any assessment of your professional development needs. We have already identified some of the management skills required (see p. 6), and here is a list of the knowledge, skills and understanding attributes. The list is not intended to be exhaustive.

Knowledge, skills and understanding about 'special educational needs' include:

- up-to-date knowledge/understanding of relevant legislation and the Code of Practice
- knowledge of a range of strategies for teaching pupils with SEN and for raising achievement
- how to select, use and evaluate appropriate forms of identification and assessment of SEN
- how to interpret the assessments of other professionals
- how to devise, write, implement and review individual education plans (IEP)
- how to plan for differentiation in the curriculum
- particular knowledge in teaching children experiencing difficulties in literacy and numeracy
- appreciation of a range of teaching and learning styles
- how to use Information and Communication Technology (ICT) to help pupils learn and gain access to the wider curriculum
- knowledge of a range of ways of involving parents in their children's education and ability to work with them as partners
- knowledge of the range of local support services and how they work with pupils with SEN
- knowledge of a range of voluntary agencies and how they support children and parents/carers
- up-to-date knowledge of research and evidence from OFSTED inspections and government reports relating to SEN

Suggestion

Identifying the knowledge, skills and attributes required by a SENCO

Use three headings: Knowledge, Skills and Attributes and make lists of those you believe to be required of a SENCO.

When you have completed the list, identify your strengths (by marking with a '+' sign) and your development needs (by a '–').

We suggest you might like to undertake the suggested Activity (see left) in order to assess your strengths and identify your professional development needs. We have carried out this activity with many SENCOs and the following table represents a list of the most common suggestions. Of course you may find many more. You may also find you categorise areas differently — this is a *personal* audit, and what is important is identifying areas and tasks.

Knowledge	Skills	Attributes
Legislation	Communication	Diplomacy
Local SEN policies and provision	Interpersonal	Calmness/Patience
Child development	Leadership	Sympathy
Different forms of SEN	Administrative	Empathy
Methods of assessment	Negotiating	Positive attitudes
How budgets work	Chairing meetings	Leadership
Parents' rights	Time management	Flexibility
Tribunal systems	Managing support assistants	Able to work cooperatively and in
National Curriculum	Report writing	collaboration with others (parent and
Teaching and Learning Styles	IEP writing	professionals)
Resources	Modifying and adapting materials	Enthusiastic/Positive
Range of intervention and teaching methods	Budget management	Confident that children can be helped
	Observation skills	Open minded
	Stress management	Approachable
	Counselling	Supportive
		Honesty and Humility

An alternative way of identifying your strengths and needs is to refer to the new National Standards and use the same method as in the Activity, that is mark them as strength (+) or need (–).

We cannot stress sufficiently the importance of assessing your own needs for further professional development. We return to this topic in the final chapter of this book. If, in fact, you have very little experience of teaching children with SEN and you also feel that you lack knowledge and skills, you are unlikely to feel confident enough to offer support to others, and you are unlikely to find 'job satisfaction' in your role. Moreover, the willingness of teachers to seek or accept advice is often related to their perceptions of the experience and 'success' of the coordinator's ability to meet SEN in their own classroom.

Having identified your own needs — how do you address them?

You must, of course, prioritise those which are of immediate personal concern. There are several sources available to you.

It is interesting to note that many teachers immediately think of their local advisory service or 'an inservice course', but consider the range of resources:

- reports on current practice in newspapers and professional journals, particularly the journals from NASEN (National Association for Special Educational Needs) — *Support for Learning* and *Special Education* and the periodical *Special Children*;
- research reports in books and journals;
- books on particular SEN topics (we have listed those we particularly recommend in the chapter on Resource Management, see p. 130), e.g. curriculum differentiation, guides to the Code of Practice, assessment, literacy and numeracy strategies;
- OFSTED inspection evidence;
- national and local assessment results, e.g. from the QCA, OFSTED, NFER and other bodies;
- booklets and information from professional associations, e.g. NASEN.
- reports and published guidelines on SEN practices from many LEAs e.g. Hampshire, Kent;
- the Internet — particularly useful to 'surf the net' for information about different disabilities;
- the SENCO Forum on the Internet. This service provides 'mutual support' for SENCOs who share experiences and information in a spirit of cooperation among SENCOs. It is particularly useful for new SENCOs. (Information about this, including joining information, is listed in Chapter 15.);
- *The SENCO Guide* (DfEE, 1997);
- inservice courses (including those leading to awards);
- courses offered by LEA, colleges and universities and other training agencies.

There are many courses available for SENCOs, but they vary considerably in that some assume participants already have experience of assessing and teaching children with SEN and they therefore emphasise interpersonal, leadership and management skills, as does this book. However, most courses of training available through LEAs and Institutions of Higher Education are of a modular structure, allowing you to select a programme of study to meet your own needs, and therefore choose modules where you can learn about assessment and teaching methods.

Supportive school structures

A good manager always offers support and encouragement to those who are 'managed' and offers praise and acknowledges their work. Smith (1982) emphasised the importance of telling colleagues who are making efforts to meet children's SEN 'how good they are'. It is also true, however, that 'managers', in this case, SENCOs, also need the same support and encouragement! You will rely heavily on your colleagues and headteacher for this, but it is also important to consider the support available through the governors — particularly the one with designated responsibility for SEN. The SEN governor can:

■ be a supportive listener who has a different perspective from that of their professional colleagues;

■ present recommendations to the governing body where appropriate;

■ present ideas to the headteacher in situations where you might lack confidence.

Of course, much depends on the expertise, professional competence and attitudes of the governor in question. It is, therefore, important that this governor receives appropriate training regarding SEN, and many LEAs provide this.

A final point to consider is that many governors do not wish to appear to be interfering in or enquiring into the professional domain of teachers. They may, therefore, be waiting to be approached to take on a more active or supportive role. If your SEN governor appears not very supportive, do not assume unwillingness or lack of interest, but invite the governor to a meeting to explore areas of possible support or to identify areas where he/she might benefit from further training. It is important to establish, from the beginning, that your major role is to *coordinate* and this involves leadership and management skills *and* an ability to work as *part of a team*.

Additional sources of information are available from a variety of non-statutory organisations such as those listed in Chapter 14.

It is important to see the whole school — headteacher, governors and colleagues — as your prime source of support.

Information about *SENCO-FORUM* is available in Chapter 15, including joining information.

Drawing up your job description and discussing how you report on your activities provides an excellent opportunity to discuss the importance and value of management support.

Summary

The role of SENCOs: What do they do?

From discussions with SEN coordinators and Designated Teachers responsible for SEN and an examination of current job and person specifications, it would seem that there are common characteristics in respect of expectations or requirements. The following is a composite list of expectations of SEN coordinators, relating to the tasks they are required to undertake.

Policy
- ensuring that the SEN policy is compatible with the individual needs of pupils
- being aware of the statutory requirements and LEA policy and ensuring that the school policy is compatible with both
- organising and contributing to policy development, review and evaluation
- informing the headteacher, governors and staff on how the school is fulfilling its legal requirements in meeting SEN
- ensuring that the SEN policy is compatible with other school policies
- ensuring that new staff are made fully aware of the school policy and procedures
- coordinating the school's SEN development plan and reporting annually to the headteacher on its progress

Procedures
- developing, maintaining and improving systems for identifying and providing for SEN
- ensuring that all concerned are aware of the procedures.
- ensuring communication systems are working effectively and efficiently.
- ensuring that the procedures for the identification, assessment, planning, provision and review of SEN are in line with the Code of Practice recommendations
- gathering information for review meetings
- organising and chairing meetings and taking minutes
- coordinating action plans and special provision

Identification, Assessment, Monitoring and Recording
- setting up and evaluating systems for the identification, assessment and monitoring of SEN
- advising and supporting colleagues on the identification and assessment of SEN

- advising and supporting colleagues on liaising with parents of pupils with SEN
- liaising with support services and agencies
- advising the headteacher on those pupils who are likely to need a statutory assessment

Provision

- discussing the educational difficulties of specific pupils with their class teachers
- advising and supporting colleagues on action planning, setting targets and developing Individual Education Programmes
- advising and supporting colleagues on providing access to a broad and balanced curriculum and differentiation strategies
- liaising with other curriculum coordinators to ensure provision for pupils with SEN across the curriculum
- keeping colleagues informed of pupils whose SEN require special provision and responding to the concerns expressed by colleagues in respect of pupils experiencing difficulties
- coordinating the provision of those who may be supporting pupils with SEN
- liaising with external services and agencies to ensure that SEN are being met
- liaising with parents and setting up partnership systems and advising and supporting colleagues in their liaison with parents and carers
- monitoring, reviewing and evaluating provision being made to meet the individual needs of pupils
- establishing close working relationships with other educational establishments in order to facilitate the transfer of pupils with SEN from one establishment to another

Resources

- maintaining and developing resources for meeting SEN
- auditing the school's resource needs
- recommending and advising colleagues on approaches, resources and their uses
- advising teachers on what resources are available in school and elsewhere and introducing new items
- discussing how resources might be used within the classroom
- keeping up to date with new developments
- managing the resources in school including setting up a resource bank and agreeing on allocation and controlling the stock
- managing the resources budget and ordering new resources

Professional development

- introducing new staff to policies, procedures and resources
- organising systems for keeping the headteacher and colleagues informed about new developments in SEN

- auditing staff needs in the area of special educational needs
- coordinating the school's SEN development plan and reporting annually to the headteacher on its progress
- planning and coordinating the school's professional development
- developing close relationships with other schools and organisations in order to exchange information, ideas and resources

From this list of expectations, the main activities appear to include:

Consulting (e.g. provision IEPs)
Advising (e.g. assessment, strategies)
Supporting (teachers, children and parents)
Setting up systems (e.g. information gathering)
Managing (e.g. support systems)
Administering (e.g. recording procedures)
Coordinating (e.g. provision, support)
Informing appropriate people (e.g. headteacher that a request is being made to proceed to statutory assessment)
Disseminating (e.g. legal requirements)
Communicating
Liaising (e.g. with appropriate agencies)
Monitoring
Reviewing
Evaluating systems, policy
Planning (e.g. professional development programmes)

Chapter 2

Leadership: Becoming a leader

Introduction

We have suggested that many Special Educational Needs Coordinators (SENCOs) in primary schools can feel particularly uncomfortable when it is suggested that they are required to manage colleagues' responses to SEN. Many primary SENCOs feel they have no supported status to encourage colleagues to 'have regard to the Code of Practice'.

Moss (1995) claims that, in practice, the distinctions between the functions of 'manager' and 'coordinator' will be more to do with the source of influence to require colleagues to get jobs done. Yet how do you get other colleagues to take on their part of the process?

You may never have thought about yourself as a 'leader'. It is important to think about your role in relation to people and to consider the influence you have in getting other people to fulfil tasks. In many primary schools, coordinators may have to rely heavily on the headteacher to provide them with the necessary authority. You may feel this to be true in your case. It is therefore necessary for you to develop your power of leadership and try to establish 'influence' through your own professional approach. In the first chapter, there was an emphasis on the need to be clear in your mind about what your responsibilities are and to think of the processes that will help you to meet them.

Being a leader

Adair (1983) suggests that it is important for a leader to have an understanding of the three areas of need which exist in working groups. Leaders, he proposes:

> ❝ . . . *should be aware of both the group and each individual, and seek to harmonise them in the service of the third factor — the common task.*   (Adair, 1983, p. 34)

He represents this by a three circle model (see Figure 2.1) which may be of use to you in developing your leadership skills.

A leader needs to be constantly aware of what is happening in the group in terms of the three areas depicted in the circles, which are always interacting with each other. Adair distinguishes between the leader having responsibility for achieving the task and at the same time having to maintain and develop the team and the individuals within it. Whilst all team members have some responsibility for the three areas, it is for the leader to appreciate that the interests of each may be at odds with the others. We suggest that you use this model to consider your leadership functions.

FIG 2.1
The Three Circles Model
(Adair, 1983)

Adair (1983) also suggests eight functions that are essential to achieving goals:

- defining the task
- planning
- briefing
- controlling
- evaluating
- motivating
- organising
- setting an example

The following checklist, based on the above functions can be used to help you to analyse the tasks ahead of you.

Defining the task: Setting the aims, objectives and purpose

- Is the task that you have been given clear or do you have a responsibility for clarifying it?
- What is the purpose of the task?
- Do you understand what has to be achieved by the task?
- Have you been given full responsibility for the implementation of the task or do you have to liaise with a member of the senior management team before reaching any decisions about the task?
- Does the task require the support of other key colleagues?
- Have these colleagues been informed by the senior management team or is it your responsibility?

Planning

- Can the task be broken down into a number of jobs?
- Do you need to include anybody else in the planning?
- Do you share the planning with colleagues so that they feel involved from the start?
- What information do you require in order to formulate your plan?
- Do you need to organise any activities to support your planning?
- Do you need the support of key personnel?
- What resources are needed to carry out the jobs and activities?

Briefing

This involves the giving out of jobs and activities, and requires the coordinator to think very carefully about how to approach the briefing session. It is crucial that you consider your behaviour towards colleagues. Points that need to be considered include:

- Are you going to delegate tasks on the basis of what has been decided at the planning stage?
- Are you going to provide opportunities for colleagues to make individual representations to you?

If the planning was done collaboratively, then the briefing stage simply involves checking that everyone is doing what they had previously agreed.

Controlling

You may not like the word controlling because it sounds rather authoritarian. However, Adair believes that an effective group or individual will become self-controlling, monitoring its own performance. The leader's aim, therefore, should be to intervene as little as possible. However, it is vital that the leader has a clear idea of:

- *what* should be happening;
- *when* it is taking place;
- *who* should be involved;
- *how* it is being done.

Evaluating

The ability to evaluate is important and it is necessary for the leader to:

- consider outcomes;
- evaluate team performance;
- appraise individuals;
- provide inservice training;
- judge the performance of colleagues.

Motivating

A leader must be sensitive to the needs and aspirations of colleagues if they are to feel motivated and committed to a task. Whitaker (1993) believes that, in any group, there are needs such as: to be supported, listened to, noticed, encouraged, trusted, appreciated and valued, informed, helped to clarify ideas, helped to develop skills and abilities, challenged and extended. It is suggested that when these needs are satisfied, people tend to work harder and with a more purposeful sense of direction. Bennett (1995) acknowledges:

 Evaluating and motivating one's colleagues, therefore, can present an acute difficulty for the educational middle manager, and along with planning shows how reconciling of task, team and individual aspirations can be difficult. (Bennett, 1995, p. 150)

Organising

In considering the organisation of your work in relation to special educational needs you need to be clear in your own mind about your responsibilities and to consider the processes that will help you to meet them. Depending upon the flexibility of your school, your organising ability will be constantly challenged by introducing changes or modifications to the system or the way that you do things. It is, therefore, essential that from time to time you review the way that you are doing things.

Setting an example

Adair believes that if you set a good example, colleagues will tend not to be too aware of it. However, they will certainly comment upon a bad example. Most people tend to say they want feedback, although it is often not well received and may even be resented. It is, therefore, helpful to subject your own behaviour to scrutiny.

Honey (1988) makes four suggestions to help you consider how you might improve your own behaviour and set a good example:
a) In situations where you do not produce the required outcome, assume that this resulted from things that you did rather than being caused by other factors. Analyse your own actions and identify those things that you might have done better.

Suggestion

Use the three circles model (p. 17) to analyse a goal you are trying to achieve in relation to your school's SEN provision. Ask the following questions:

Task needs
1. What is the common task?
2. How is it communicated to everyone?

Team needs
3. Who is in the team/working group?
4. How do they contribute to the purpose?
5. How do they relate together as a team?

Individual needs
6. Do the individual parts have maximum possible freedom and discretion?
7. In what ways are the needs of the individuals being met?

Suggestion

Leadership style

Think of any situation in which you have had a leadership role.
1. How did you feel? How did you behave towards those in your team?
2. Do you prefer to work in a highly structured way, where roles and tasks are clearly assigned to people? Do you like to work in open 'free-wheeling' situations? In which situations do you feel most confident?
3. How do you respond to an individual in the team who may be unable (or say they are unable) to participate fully because of other demands? To what extent does your concern for people outweigh your concern for the task?

b) In situations where you do produce the required outcomes, occasionally review your actions to see if you might have performed better.
c) In situations where you are upset by other colleague's reactions, assume that it is your fault.
d) In situations where you do receive critical feedback about your behaviour try to accept it gratefully rather than becoming defensive. Feedback is useful if you know that you can do something constructive with the information provided.

Leading a team

Crucial to the concept of implementing the SEN Code of Practice, and making whole school policies work, is the concept of teamwork. No matter how enthusiastic and committed you are to improving SEN practices, provision of a high quality involves the cooperation and commitment of all the staff. You must, therefore, be realistic in what you ask — there may be implications for some staff may be needing to change attitudes or acquire new skills. Undoubtedly there are likely to be members of staff with varied experiences, knowledge and personalities: some will be more receptive to change than others; some may have considerably more experience of teaching children with SEN than you have. It is important to consider the staff as a major resource. Belbin (1981) concluded that a successful team is composed of people taking on diverse roles, with a range of ideas, personal styles, interests and abilities, and that it is the interaction of these differences which can lead to successful outcomes.

It is important for you to be able to analyse your own ideas of leadership and teamwork. A team is effective when it achieves the goals set by means which have been agreed by all members. The development of a school policy, where all staff feel a sense of ownership, is one example of such teamwork. An effective leader, as Adair suggests, will have concern for both the task ahead and the people involved. It may be that some leaders are unable to maintain a balance. The suggested activity may help you to consider whether you can keep 'a balance'.

It is often difficult, when working in a team, to be aware of how the group is working. As a SENCO, you may see yourself both as leader of a team, and also working within one: you will lead developments of policies and practices within your school, and lead or coordinate a small team each time you are involved in developing and monitoring a child's IEP. Moss (1995) draws attention to the fact that you may also have:

 . . . additional specialist support for named children. There will be non-teaching assistants, parent volunteers, older students, and peers (e.g. as mentors in paired reading schemes) who may be used to support special needs work. (Moss, 1995, p. 3)

The majority of SENCOs do manage a group of special needs workers. However, this group may, unlike that of other subject coordinators, comprise a diverse group of full-time, part-time, temporary, qualified, unqualified, teaching and non-teaching staff. Have you considered how you support your team, however small it might be? The main issue in managing such a group is maintaining coherence and ensuring that individuals within it are not marginalised. Whatever the composition of the team it is necessary for all members to appreciate 'teampeopleship'.

You will also be a vital member of a multi-professional team involving professionals from a range of external agencies and including a child's parents and carers. Such teams may appear all the more diverse because members come together for a specific task, but bring with them very different forms of training, resources, concerns about status and knowledge. Moreover, you may find yourself at times leading this team (e.g. at a Case Conference in school) or being led by another professional (e.g. when you contribute to a meeting chaired by an LEA officer).

Primary schools provide little opportunity for practising working in a team with adults because so much of a teacher's work is with children in the classroom, but effective teamwork is essential to an effective school.

What are the characteristics of an effective team?

- tasks are successfully achieved
- the working environment is relaxed and supportive enabling people to say what they think, to listen to one another and develop each other's ideas
- people trust each other, agree the objectives and are fully committed to achieving the objectives
- people learn from experience and regularly review their performance as part of their work
- conflict is minimal because it is worked through and decisions are reached by consensus
- leadership/coordination is shared as appropriate
- members of the team function in various but complementary ways

You might wish to compare this list with the characteristics of ineffective teams:

- atmosphere strained or bored
- ideas and personal feelings suppressed for fear of criticism
- discussion often irrelevant, may be dominated by one/two individuals
- behaviour issues and progress are not reviewed
- no evidence of common objectives
- conflict either avoided or develops into open warfare
- decisions made by majority votes rather than consensus
- people do not listen to each other
- leader/coordinator maintains tight control.

It is interesting to look at these lists and realise that they are also the characteristics of effective and ineffective classrooms.

You could use a team meeting as an occasion for analysing how effectively your team is working. Ask one member to act as 'detached' observer, with the responsibility of providing feedback to the team. He or she could use the grid below to 'categorise' each team member's behaviours during a planning meeting (without identifying names).

These categories are taken from the work of Rackham et al. (1971), Honey (1988) and Everard and Morris (1996). It is possible to add other categories or devise other checklists, depending on the type of behaviours or contributions you wish to analyse. It is important not to imply that some behaviours are 'good' and others 'bad'. There may be times, for example, when it is necessary to state and clarify the nature of

Behaviour	Team Members					
	1	2	3	4	5	6
Seeking views (Asking others for their ideas)						
Proposing (Making proposals, forwarding ideas)						
Suggesting (Forwarding ideas as questions, e.g. Should we . . . ? How about doing . . . ?)						
Agreeing (Supporting what others have said)						
Stating Difficulties (Pointing out problems, e.g. 'I don't agree with that,' 'We don't have enough time' etc.)						
Seeking Clarification (Summarising to gain understanding, requesting further information, e.g. 'Could you develop it further?', 'Do you mean . . . ?)						
Clarifying (Giving explanations and information)						
Interrupting (Everyone speaks at once or breaking in to stop someone finishing their contribution)						

difficulties and obstacles. What is important is to see team members *sharing* contributions across categories, and to be able to deal with anyone who continually states difficulties in order to obstruct development. Observing a team at work provides opportunities to consider several aspects of teamwork and can help individuals and particular leaders to change their behaviour to support the needs of the team.

Effective teams are important but we should remind you that teams are not always necessary: you will need to identify which of your tasks are more demanding and therefore require a high level of teamwork.

Colleagues are likely to be more supportive and cooperative if they know that their expertise or skills will only be called upon when crucial to the successful achievement of a problem or task but not on a regular basis for more routine activities which do not necessarily require their participation.

Developing teams

A team does not necessarily develop smoothly, and Leigh and Maynard (1995) suggest that there are six stages of team development which you might find useful when working in any of the teams you are involved with — whole school staff (to encourage all staff to meet their pupils' SEN); a small team of learning support assistants; a small, multi-professional team.

- Starting
- Sorting
- Stabilising
- Striving
- Succeeding
- Stopping

Starting stage

When a team meets together for the first time some people may feel anxious, particularly if they have not worked with each other before or are concerned about how effective they will be. It is essential that time is made available for getting to know each other. Activities should be organised which enable those present to identify what they feel they can contribute to the team and to help reduce interpersonal barriers. It is helpful to set conditions for open exchanges of information to take place and develop 'trust-building'. As the SENCO you may set the example by making some positive contributions and encouraging members to identify tasks in areas where they feel confident.

Sorting stage

This can be a difficult and uncomfortable stage as colleagues start seeking clarification about the task, their roles and their powers. It is advisable to let disagreements and conflicts come to the surface. Opportunities need to be provided for resolving relationship problems and to help in dealing with conflict constructively. It is during this period that agreement should be reached about individual roles and boundaries.

Stabilising stage

This is usually the stage at which there is growing clarity about what is to be achieved and how it is going to be done. Colleagues become more aware of their roles and responsibilities and of what other team members are doing. The team may decide to formalise its task allocation. It is generally felt that better teams are those which enable people to work flexibly and contribute in a variety of ways. At this stage colleagues feel more reassured as uncertainties are resolved and the team starts to enjoy positive working relationships.

Striving stage

The team reaches a performing stage where it starts to achieve results. It is now considered to be a competent team. However, it is necessary to look for signs of waning enthusiasm. It is important to give regular feedback and consider the progress that is being made. Leigh and Maynard (1995) suggest that an essential feature to look for in a striving team is its ability to handle risk.

Succeeding stage

Not all teams reach this stage — a succeeding team is one which consistently achieves outstanding results and makes the best use of everyone's potential. People in these teams thrive on autonomy and challenge rather than being directed or controlled. In these teams it is often difficult to identify the leader because everyone tends to adopt leader-like behaviour. To motivate and inspire a succeeding team requires support in the form of training and development which enables team members to become more creative and proactive.

Stopping stage

Effective teams seldom last forever. Sometimes they may stop and then start again in a new form. This may happen because the task is complete or because some members leave, roles change or a new challenge revitalises it. When a team does come to an end it should celebrate its achievement or formally mark its ending by reviewing what has been achieved and the roles that individual members have played.

It is clear from this that good interpersonal and 'people-management' skills are important, and these are considered later. It is useful, however, to try to improve your skills in managing teams purposefully. Where a team is going to continue to work together (i.e. it has not been brought together to achieve a single task) it is useful to carry out a short review or evaluation — involving, of course, all team members.

Reviewing Teamwork

Ask all team members to complete this short rating inventory following completion of a task which the group has worked on. Put a mark on the line to show how you rate the element.

I. Do you think the team achieved its goal?

Not at all..Completely

2. Were the objectives set clearly?

Unclear...Very clear

3. Was the task defined clearly?

Unclear...Very clear

4. Were all members of the team involved in planning what should be done?

No...All involved

5. Did all members know what was expected of them?

Not clearly...All knew clearly

6. Did every member play a full part?

No..Fully involved

7. Was the team led effectively?

Ineffective...Very effective

8. Was progress monitored?

Not noticeably..Very well

9. How do you feel about the outcomes of the teamwork?

Dissatisfied..Very satisfied

10. Any other comments (e.g. major strengths of the team, areas for improvement)

....

....

Managing change

Leadership often involves introducing change — to implement new policies, improve practices as a result of evaluation and to introduce new methods and approaches to teaching. The very word 'change' is highly emotive to teachers who have seen so many changes since the Education Reform Act of 1988 and the advent of (and modifications to) the National Curriculum. All too often change means an increased workload.

As all schools now have a policy for SEN and should be working with regard to the Code of Practice. It is unlikely that you will be involved in the sort of major change this brought to many schools. What you must always be involved in is the change needed to improve practices: in some cases this may be to facilitate processes and reduce workload!

Managing change calls on your skills of leadership to persuade staff to want to be involved in a process, for successful change is only likely to occur when teachers:
■ perceive the need for it (and believe in it);
■ understand the purpose and goal;
■ feel fully involved in bringing it about (ownership).

A major test of your leadership is to be able to *identify a need*. Fullan (1991) pointed to the futility of some change brought about by those

> ❝ . . . *skilled at managing change, but empty-headed about what changes are most needed.* (Fullan, 1991, p. 5)

All change needs planning, controlling, monitoring and action planning. It should be seen as a continuous process of development rather than something that is done only when things are not going too well. There is no universal model so it is necessary for you to identify a model of organisational change which you can use comfortably. This model should comprise a mixture of your personal values, beliefs, feelings, opinions and perceptions. So where do you start?

Let us consider a model for change management. Unless you are able to define *why* there is a need for change, and your colleagues can clearly understand *why* and *how* they need to change then there may only be a half-hearted commitment to the process. It is the attitude of your colleagues which will have the greatest influence on the success of any proposed change. As a manager you must create opportunities in which colleagues feel able to share their views, needs and aspirations and clarify the reason for change. It is also necessary to analyse the current position and what effect this is having in the school.

This should then be followed by an examination of how the school might respond, what methods are available and identification of the various roles required to support successful change. A cautionary point is that when any organisation faces change they often believe that *everything* will have to be new. In most situations, however, there will be some existing effective/successful practices. You are, therefore, encouraged to *evaluate* the past and *identify key features* which might be kept or further developed. This evaluation may also reassure colleagues that there are examples of past practice which are valued and worth keeping. Not only does this appear to reduce some of the threat of change, but it also raises morale when past endeavours are acknowledged as effective or successful.

Unfortunately, no matter how carefully you try to introduce change, some people may feel threatened or insecure. This may be because they can point to their successes with particular practices, or they may be uncertain as to their ability to meet new demands, or they may feel that the very essence of their professional identity is being questioned. An example of a major change in which you will be involved is the greater emphasis now given to the use of ICT (Information and Communications Technology). Whilst some teachers are highly skilled in using ICT within their classroom, others have made little use of it and their training needs can make them feel uncomfortable and even incompetent. Similarly, the emphasis on improving primary teachers' subject knowledge at Key Stage 2, particularly in literacy, maths and science has made some teachers feel 'de-skilled'. The TTA's strategy in helping teachers to identify their professional development needs in relation to this knowledge has been to commission the production of materials which can be used by individual teachers without a need to expose any inadequacies publicly. This strategy then relies on professional integrity for individuals to seek to redress any gaps in knowledge, or for schools and LEAs to make provision in an open, supportive and non-threatening way.

In planning change, a leader must call upon good interpersonal skills, demonstrate an appreciation of colleagues' feelings and not be surprised if proposals are met by resistance.

It is possible to summarise the main reasons for resistance to change in the workplace as arising from any one or combination of the following:
■ professional disagreement;
■ loss of the past;
■ fear of the future;
■ dislike of 'the management' (school, government, the 'bringer' of change);
■ personal problems.

Plant (1987) suggests that resistance takes two forms: systematic and behavioural. *Systematic* resistance comes about because of the lack of: relevant information; managerial ability; knowledge and skills. *Behavioural* resistance characterises resistance which results from reactions, perceptions and assumptions of both individuals and groups within the organisation. It is obviously a little easier to deal with a complaint about poor communication than with an emotion-based resistance such as low self-esteem. It is imperative not to ignore resistance because it could lead to serious consequences later on in the process. Leigh (1988) suggests that it may be more appropriate to consider 'actions to reduce rather than eliminate resistance' and offers some examples of actions that may be used.

The following are some examples of emotions and behaviours that may be displayed at times of resistance:

Aggression	— having tantrums, making verbal attacks, being rude and showing anger.
Playing	— using humour, being sarcastic and being nonchalant.
Withdrawing	— avoiding issues and becoming isolated from colleagues.
Competing	— attention seeking.
Seeking sympathy	— 'You have far more experience than me!'
Blocking	— being argumentative, uncooperative and not meeting deadlines.
Subvert	— agitating and undermining authority.

Once you have recognised some of the warning signs of resistance then it may be helpful to arrange an interview with the colleague(s) concerned if you would like to help them. Provide a structure for the interview and consider the interpersonal communication skills discussed in Chapter 3 (see p. 40).

Action — planning for change

A useful method of planning programmes of action is to use Lewin's force-field analysis. This method may be used by an individual, with a critical friend or with a group. Its purpose is to distinguish between the positive (facilitating) and negative (restraining) aspects of a situation and then to consider how you might overcome the negative influences. The steps in the process are:

a) Define the change that is desired — What do you want to happen?
b) Identify the reasons for the change — Why is it happening?
c) Compare the relevant factors — Identify the positive and negative factors:
   positive factors   negative factors
   (List five factors that could be beneficial to the situation)
   (List five factors that could be detrimental to the situation)
d) Consider methods of minimising the negative factors — How can these negative factors be lessened?
e) What strategies can be implemented to maximise the positive factors and reduce the negative factors?
f) These strategies then form the basis of a detailed action plan.

Keep the plan as simple as possible and ensure that it is clear about the tasks required, who will do what and by when, and the resources that will be needed to support it. Establish criteria for each of the tasks so that you may determine when they have been successfully achieved. The use of force-field analysis with a group helps members to reach a common understanding of the situation, develop a sense of teamwork and initiate group commitment to a common objective.

FIG 2.2
A model for planning for change

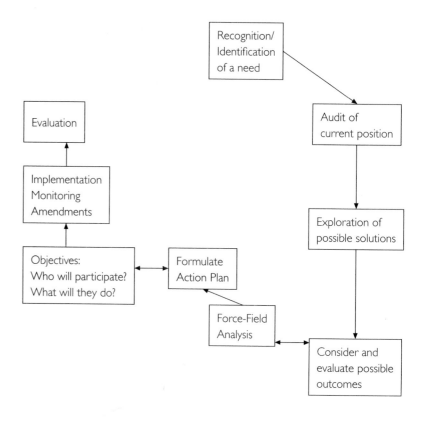

An example of how you might use the model

1. Identifying the need
It may be that you believe some aspect of SEN provision is
not working effectively — or not being carried out as well as
it might be (e.g. maintaining Individual Education Plans).
What evidence is there to support your concern?
a) It is essential to talk to the headteacher about your concern.
b) Find out as much as you can (don't assume that you know
   what is happening). Can you find *good* examples? Is your
   own practice good? Collect information: examples of
   children's work, opinions of staff, any relevant records and
   documentation, opinions of parents.

2. Audit of current position
a) Find out about practices elsewhere. What advice
   do local and national bodies provide about this area,
   e.g. OFSTED, QCA, the LEA? What does the law say? What
   advice is there in the Code of Practice? What do
   professional associations and journals offer as an example

of requirements and good practice? Can you find out about practices in other schools?

b) What are the views of
- parents?
- pupils?
- governors?
- support service personnel?

c) What documentary evidence have you in your school?

3. Inform staff and governors of the goal of your proposed change
How will parents be informed?

4. Persuading the staff of the need
a) Discuss the matter first with the headteacher and gain support.
   You need to be able to convince staff by:
   - informing them about the reasons for the change:
     — legal requirements;
     — children's needs not being identified;
     — underachievement;
     — parental concerns.
   - demonstrating how you have worked successfully using the 'preferred' methods (or be able to point to others who have done so)
   - inviting someone from another school to talk about their experience of this area
   - explaining how it will affect (beneficially) all aspects of teaching and learning, emphasising how it will improve learning opportunities for children.
   You must be able to show them the possible solutions and implications (as a result of step 2a).
b) Draw up your force-field analysis and consider how to move forward.

5. Action Planning
We suggest you use Adair's model in planning and evaluating what you do. Everyone needs to be clear about:
- who is leading the plan;
- the role and task of each person concerned;
- resources available;
- the timescale;
- the desired outcome.

6. Monitoring and reviewing progress
If the action plan has been carefully drawn up then you should find it easy to monitor progress. Where problems arise you might revisit the force-field analysis to help identify difficulties and strategies.

7. Evaluation
This must be built in at the planning stage — in fact, taking responsibility for leading an evaluation is a significant dimension of a coordinator's role.

Managing evaluation

Perhaps one of your most important duties as a SENCO is to review and evaluate your school's SEN policies and practices — we have devoted Chapter 5 to this. However, there are some general principles to evaluation which you need to consider so that you can apply them to various aspects of SEN provision. You will find that submitting evaluation reports to staff, headteacher, governors and parents helps to reinforce the status of your role and reminds everyone of the importance of meeting children's SEN.

Evaluation addresses the question of the value of what is being done. It may be concerned with 'Does a process/practice achieve its aim?' or it may lead to the question of 'how well' it meets a need. You may be involved in evaluating processes and practices or evaluating materials for use with children with SEN. We deal with the latter aspect in the chapter on resources.

It is important to develop a systematic approach to the evaluation process, a key decision being the extent to which you lead but share responsibility for the evaluation with others, or whether you assume sole responsibility. The stages of the process are the same whether it is a single or joint undertaking.

An evaluation is, of course, a starting point in determining a further change process. Evaluations vary in terms of scale, but the same process will be required, and you might like to carry out a small-scale evaluation before undertaking a review of the whole SEN policy!

The evaluation process

Planning
What is the purpose of the evaluation? Who wants it to be carried out and why?
What is the subject matter of the evaluation?
When is it to be carried out?
Who will be involved (responsible for the evaluation? (i.e. members of the evaluation team)
Who will report on findings — and how (writing/oral report) and to whom?
What kinds of information/evidence will be collected? How? From whom? Is confidentiality an issue?

Introducing the process
How are you keeping staff informed about the evaluation — its purpose and the way it might impinge on their time/teaching?
Are they aware of your expectations of their involvement?
Inform them of your methods of collecting data, e.g. observation, records, interviews, etc.

Collecting information
What forms of data are you collecting?
Carry out observations, analyses of documents, etc. If you decide you need information sources not previously identified, make sure you go back to the staff to obtain agreement (and justify the change!).

Analysing the information
How are you going to analyse and present the information?
You might look for recurring themes/areas.
Try to distinguish between facts and opinions offered by those giving information. In particular try *not* to offer your *interpretation* at this stage.
Can you use tables, diagrams, graphs to present information?

Reporting your results
Whether you provide an oral or written report, it is important to give a structured account, e.g.
Introduction
- the subject/topic of evaluation
- purpose of the evaluation
- who the report has been prepared for (target audience)
Key issues
- focus of the evaluation
- criteria used to make judgments

Methods
- how the information was collected — from whom, using what methods?
- how the information was analysed

Presentation of findings
- data
- main results

Conclusions

Recommendations (not always required, but often useful)

Chapter 3

Managing and supporting people: Developing good communication and interpersonal skills

Introduction

It is clear that a SENCO has to be able to work effectively with a range of people from diverse backgrounds who bring varying experiences and expectations to any contact with the SENCO. These include pupils, their parents, teachers who work in the same primary school, learning support assistants, visiting teachers from external support services, other professionals such as speech therapists, educational psychologists and social workers, administrators and SEN Advisers. It is not unusual for a SENCO in a primary school to have contact with 30–40 different professionals, only 6 of whom may be on the school staff. It is important therefore, to be able to work collaboratively, supportively and purposefully. Central to this will be the need for effective communication.

It is worth thinking about the fact that communication always implies a two-way process, whether *spoken* (and listened to) or *written* (and read). This fundamental aspect is often overlooked, but there are major implications:
- a communicator has to ensure that a receiver (listener or reader) can *understand* what it is that is being communicated. There are implications here for tone, language used (including jargon) and an appreciation of the pre-existing knowledge, experiences and attitudes of the recipient, because these will all affect how (or even whether) the message is received;

How effective is communication in your school? What are your main responsibilities for communication?

- a communicator requires feedback;
- participants in communication must adopt both roles: how often have you heard the complaint 'The communication in this school's awful' or 'The (LEA) Offices never let us know'?

It is important for you, as a coordinator (the very word implies communication) to evaluate the effectiveness of communication in your school, particularly in relation to SEN. The major purposes of communication within a school are both

- *task oriented*:
  — to help staff share a common vision;
  — to facilitate teamwork by being equally well informed;
  — to aid consistency in practices;
  — to inform staff, governors, parents and others about policies and practices, pupils' progress, new ideas and developments.
- *social/emotional oriented*:
  — to develop and maintain good social relationships;
  — to encourage the development of trust and high self-esteem.

Communication will vary depending on:

- *purpose* of the communication (to inform, persuade, advise, etc.) and
- *the person/people* with whom you communicate (pupils, colleagues, other professionals, governors, parents, etc.)

Effective interpersonal communication is often supported by clear, written communication/documentation, particularly where a major purpose has been to inform. It is important, therefore, that you develop a good communication system and that you evaluate it regularly. Silence is not a sign that it is working. It is essential to obtain feedback. Poor communication can lead to misunderstandings, non-compliance with school policies and practices, apparent lack of interest and feelings of alienation.

It may be useful to devise a communication plan. Begin by identifying how information currently flows upward, downward and laterally within school and then externally, both from and into the school. This will help you to clarify to whom each person in the school is responsible and who is accountable for what. It will also provide you with an opportunity to find out if there are any situations for which there is no official communication procedure or if there is a colleague who is not receiving relevant information. It may be useful to draw up systems for both the collection and dissemination of information. A communication plan might include the following headings:

a) who is responsible
b) target group
c) information required, and in what format
d) distribution process
e) resources required
f) method of evaluation and obtaining feedback.

You should also evaluate how effective the communication about the school's SEN policy and practices has been. Moss (1995) suggests using a simple questionnaire or checklist to help you to clarify what staff understand about the Code of Practice and what they require of you. In order to obtain support from staff they need to have clear information. However, a note of caution — designing a questionnaire is not quite as simple as it may first appear. You should consider what information you want and how you are going to make use of it. Factual information may sometimes be obtained by using simple 'Yes or No' questions. However, if you wish colleagues to elaborate upon their response then you may need to consider the use of open questions. Care should be taken over presentation, layout, and the instructions, including a date for its return. Thought should also be given as to whether you require the names of respondents or whether they may remain anonymous. A useful resource is SCRE (*Using Questionnaires in Small-Scale Research: A Teacher's Guide*). It may also be worthwhile to include a personal note of appreciation and an offer to circulate the results of the exercise to those interested. We have all responded to questionnaires. How often are our efforts recognised?

The results of such a survey should provide you with an overview of the level of understanding about the Code of Practice and help you prepare for the next stage of deciding the most effective strategy for communicating information about areas of concern, ambiguity or lack of knowledge. Moss (1995) suggests that such a survey may help you identify the need for such things as particular INSET activities, the production of briefing sheets or identification of liaison systems.

You could also use a similar short questionnaire to find out how much parents and governors understand about the school's practices for meeting SEN. This will lead to a re-examination of the documentation provided for governors and parents and the strategies you use for communications, particularly with parents. Have efforts been made to provide user-friendly information and to welcome enquiries? What efforts have been made to meet the needs of any parents whose home language is not English?

> A useful resource in examining written communication between school and home may be found in Bastiani (1978).

Interpersonal skills

Although communicating clearly and simply in writing is very important, it tends to be very formal and good interpersonal communication skills are the most effective means of ensuring understanding, cooperation and development.

Interpersonal skills for effective coordinators

- respect for colleagues' and others' views
- active and passive listening skills
- clear, consistent presentation of ideas
- giving positive and constructive feedback
- openness to ideas and able to accept negative feedback from others
- problem solving and decision making
- able to be assertive and maintain composure
- able to handle conflict/manage 'difficult' people
- persuasive and negotiating behaviours and language

Respect for others

'Mutual respect' is a significant feature in cooperative developments. Respect for your colleagues, parents and others may be shown in a variety of ways such as being sensitive to the time and place when you approach them; paying them attention when speaking to them; listening to them without interruption; not passing negative value judgments on their opinions, practices and ideas; being prepared, at times, to adopt a compromise; not trying to impose your views on them. In particular, it is important that negative non-verbal communicative behaviours do not belie any positive statements you may utter. Holding eye-contact, smiling appropriately (occasionally mirroring the others' expressions — if someone is particularly upset, you should not have a wide grin on your face!), and not signalling boredom or that your attention is wandering, are all important facets of supportive communication. Think of the signals of respect or value for others which are sent by laughing, using a sarcastic comment or looking at your watch when people are talking of something of central importance to them!

Effective listening

Effective listening embraces several skills. It involves preparation to empathise with a speaker and an attempt to see the world or topic of communication from the speaker's viewpoint. It also involves listening to pieces of information, analysing the significant parts of a message (often having to re-organise them), relating the information to existing knowledge or understanding and being able to check on understanding. A good listener facilitates communication using certain strategies.

Communication should take place in a facilitative environment. Very often a SENCO is being asked for advice or given information which may be of a very personal nature, whether by pupils, parents or colleagues. This means that the speaker may be in a vulnerable position, concerned, upset or emotionally troubled in some way. It is important to establish an appropriate climate in a setting where there are unlikely to be any disturbances from telephones or pupils or adults interrupting. The latter can be prevented by putting a 'Please do not disturb' notice on the door. Certain skills and actions contribute towards establishing an appropriate climate:

- sitting near each other without barriers, e.g. a desk;
- using a relaxed posture;

- welcoming expressions including facial expressions and welcoming gestures;
- using specific strategies which encourage speakers to continue, e.g. 'Hmm', 'That's okay', 'Yes', 'Aha', in a soft, low tone;
- allowing for comfortable silences;
- not interfering;
- offering openings like 'This seems to be worrying you', 'How are things going?'

It is possible to distinguish between *passive listening*, which usually implies listening to a speaker without interrupting other than to show you are attending, and *active listening*. Active listening skills are very important for SENCOs, as this definition suggests:

 ... the listener attempts to gain insights into the perceptual, intellectual and emotional world of the speaker ... any concerns of the listener are temporarily suspended.

(Whittaker, 1994, p. 59)

Very often when pupils, parents or colleagues approach a SENCO they have not necessarily been able to identify their anxieties or concerns. They may, therefore, need to have an active listener who can help them clarify and explore their concerns and sources of anxiety. An active listener not only demonstrates attention is being paid to what the speaker says by using the skills listed earlier, but also encourages them to continue, by:

- respecting silences, giving the speaker time to reflect;
- avoiding a tendency to 'jump in' to fill a silence;
- repeating a phrase, nodding, smiling;
- demonstrating an attempt to understand by reflecting back to them what they have said, thereby also helping them to clarify their thoughts;
- paraphrasing a statement;
- summarising periodically;
- making a statement referring to the speaker's feelings and emotions about the topic or a situation that has been described, e.g. 'You felt confused because one report said she/he was doing well and then the next report said she/he was underachieving.'

This not only legitimises feelings, but also enables the speaker to reconsider both the emotion ('No, I felt angry and that the teachers weren't competent,' may be a response) and the reasons they gave ('Well, the information wasn't very precise').

There are certain key points to remember:

■ Avoid interrupting.

■ Avoid saying 'I understand completely' (you *can't* and this may be perceived as *lack* of understanding).

■ Avoid giving a quick 'solution' to what has been a major problem for someone.

■ Avoid trying to tell the speaker about your problems and concerns. Sometimes you may be tempted to do this as a way of demonstrating that you know what it's like to experience problems, but it is usually interpreted as showing a lack of care and understanding of the speaker's concerns.

■ Try to avoid passing judgments!

What active listeners do, in a subtle way, is to allow the speaker an opportunity to explore their own feelings and clarify their situation in a way which empowers them to share in any subsequent decisions and take responsibility for themselves.

Clear and consistent presentation of ideas

There are skills to be learned for you as speaker/communicator. The following suggestions should help you to convey your message/ideas:

■ *Plan ahead what you are going to say*:
  — state the purpose of the communication clearly and inform the person/people of this purpose before you meet with them, if possible (so that they meet you with some knowledge and perceptions of what to expect and have had some time to prepare), *or* at the outset of the discussion (this will help you and them to keep to the point and understand what sort of outcomes there should be)
  — think about the language you will use: will it be familiar to, and easily understood by, the recipient? (Language can be a barrier to communication.)

— plan any arguments so that they are logically presented, without too much emotive/value-laden language: be consistent in your arguments

— consider using concrete materials where appropriate to help illustrate what you are saying (for example, if you are introducing new materials for teaching, *show* them, and, if possible, work produced by their children as a result of using them; show parents examples of their children's work rather than just talking about it)

■ *During your discussions*:

— Provide opportunities for questions and seek feedback to check understanding

— Be a good listener

— Be prepared to compromise where this will be at least a step *towards* a desired end (i.e. this is a 'strategic compromise')

— Summarise the conclusions at the end of any encounter, particularly in terms of any implications for action (*who* will do *what*, by *when*)

— Consider providing a written summary of the conclusions either at the end of the meeting or shortly after. This is a reminder of any action to be taken and also offers a further opportunity for the person/people with whom you were communicating to challenge/agree with the outcome. This is particularly important if you have been communicating with someone who was upset, angry or concerned during the encounter as their emotional state could affect their perception of the communication.

Giving positive and constructive feedback

There are two forms of feedback: positive and negative. Negative feedback implies either a rejection of someone's actions and statements, or a negative evaluation of their behaviours. Positive feedback, as you know from your teaching, implies offering praise for effort and achievement and offers constructive advice for further development. Constructive feedback does not imply that there are no problems or difficulties, and, in fact, a difficult situation in giving feedback is when a person has acted inappropriately and it is your role as coordinator to ask or show them how to act more appropriately. It is necessary in this case for you to focus on the *act* and not on the *person*. This may be relatively simple when supporting teachers, for example, in improving their writing of IEP, but more difficult when you are discussing their interactions with pupils presenting them with behavioural difficulties.

Giving feedback requires sensitivity to the feelings of the recipient and being able to recommend a range of possible solutions, leaving it to the individual to take responsibility for choosing their own response. It is much better to give constructive feedback in person, rather than writing (e.g. letters, notes or memos) where the tone may be more formal and you cannot respond to the recipient's interpretation of the message.

Feedback is important, not only to understand communication has been understood, but to extend and develop relationships and ideas. What we know about positive feedback is that it fosters personal growth and increases achievement and self-esteem. It reduces uncertainty and low morale. As a SENCO you will often be dealing with people (pupils, parents and colleagues) who have low self-esteem and who may feel uncertain about their own ability — as a learner, a parent or teacher of pupils with SEN. It is important, therefore, that you transfer your proven ability for positive teaching to your work with adults to build their confidence. In all your interactions you need to take some time to acknowledge and point out to colleagues their strengths and competencies, as a basis for helping them to develop further. Trethowan (1989) states that good feedback:

- is specific
- is descriptive
- is clearly expressed
- is well timed
- takes into account the needs of the receiver
- concentrates on things people can do something about.

All of this means you must try to learn as much as you can (from observing, talking and listening to) about the people you work with, in order to show consideration for their feelings and a genuine appreciation of their strengths.

Being open to ideas and accepting negative feedback

Receiving negative feedback, on the other hand, tends to leave a person feeling undervalued, insecure and even threatened. A reaction to this might be to reject anything the person who gave this feedback says in future, to feel antagonistic towards him or her, or — particularly if the recipient rarely receives any positive feedback — reducing their self-esteem. The effect of negative feedback, therefore, is that people retreat into themselves, do not 'take risks', and creativity, development and growth are inhibited. Yet as a SENCO, you need to be able to lead others and take calculated risks if you are to develop the role and opportunities for pupils with SEN. A leader has to learn to deal with negative feedback from others as much as offering positive feedback to others. People who feel vulnerable are often likely to offer negative feedback. Understanding this fact will often help you to understand why you may be at the receiving end — to many of the people you deal with you appear in a 'stronger' (emotionally, intellectually and professionally) position.

Strategies for coping with negative feedback:
- Ask yourself why the feedback was negative — did you do or say something that *was* inappropriate? If 'yes', should you apologise, *or* consider how you can redress the situation *or* behave differently in future? If 'no', then why do you think it was perceived negatively? How can you redress the situation?
- Consider your strengths and competencies to 'counter balance' the negative.
- Set yourself some positive targets which will rise above the negative information.

Although some writers would say that all leaders should be 'thick-skinned' and learn to 'ignore' and *expect* negative feedback because of their position which inevitably offers challenges to people, we do not agree. It is always worth asking the question *why*, but then taking some positive action. What is counter-productive is to dwell on the negative which will lower your self-esteem.

It is also to be hoped that your colleagues, the parents and pupils, and in particular your headteacher and governors, recognise your work as a SENCO and offer plenty of positive, constructive feedback. A good senior manager will be aware of the need to praise the middle management. Above all, learn to recognise and acknowledge your own successes!

Problem solving and decision making

This area has been considered as part of teamwork and action planning (see p. 25). Many may look to you to make decisions, and there may be times when you will have major responsibility for making a decision. However, there are certain key elements:

- Involve all interested parties in decision making where the outcome will affect them.
- Brief people fully — prepare documentation where necessary and share problems: if you are holding a meeting allow time before or at the start of the meeting for them to prepare ideas.
- Create an atmosphere of trust where everyone can share their views (using your communication skills) — you may need to arrange the seating in a room so that everyone can see each other.
- Do not begin a discussion about problem solving by suggesting that you have already decided what should happen.
- Encourage brainstorming, where everyone feels able to offer ideas or 'solutions' which are not evaluated at the time (have these written on a flipchart or on cards).
- Consider possible suggestions and solutions, seeking views about possible consequences. (This can be done by just talking through some of the ideas or by writing them down and listing consequences which can then be rated as positive or negative according to the perceived advantages or disadvantages.) The emphasis must be on considering the *ideas* not identifying individuals with the suggestion. This usually means that people are more prepared to participate and will generate more potential solutions.
- Your role is to participate and chair, not to be arbiter.

- Determine whether the decision will be based on consensus, a vote, left to a small number of people to reach a consensus or left to you to take a decision.
- Summarise the decision made and make sure that everyone has felt they have been involved/consulted, even if they are unhappy with the decision.
- Clarify the next part of an action plan including how that action will be monitored and reviewed.

Being assertive

Learning to be assertive requires practice. It means that you will be confident in making your views known without offending others or being aggressive. An aggressive person tends to dominate and may well intimidate others, whereas an assertive person implies consistency to one's beliefs and views, but flexible in terms of negotiation and communication with others. As a SENCO you will often find yourself in situations of conflicting interests (for example, you may make a case for a pupil with SEN to be taught within your school although other teachers may wish to exclude him/her).

Assertiveness is about feeling confident *and being able to*:
- be honest with yourself and others;
- express your point of view clearly, making sure that you are listened to;
- make other people aware of what you can and cannot do within the time allocated;
- acknowledge the concerns of others;
- inform people when you feel you have impossible demands made on you and how you are feeling;
- allow yourself to make mistakes;
- give precise advice, information and guidelines to others and respect their interests and feelings;
- listen effectively and provide constructive feedback;
- respect other people and their right to be assertive;
- control the volume and tone of your voice (don't shout);
- keep calm and control your emotions;
- avoid arguments (ask for more time to 'think about it').

You can practise being assertive — particularly if you feel inclined to either aggressive or submissive behaviour in certain types of difficult situations — by looking at the types of words or phrases used in conversations, for example:

- *Differentiate between fact and opinion*, e.g. I find it difficult to . . . , In my opinion . . . , I see it like this. . . .
- *Use open-ended questions* when finding out about the views of others, e.g. How are you? What are your thoughts on . . . ?
- *Look for resolutions to problems*, e.g. Is there a way round this? How does this sound?
- *Refrain* from using words like 'should', 'must', 'have to' and 'ought'.

Managing conflict

As a SENCO there will inevitably be some time when you may find yourself having to manage conflict or deal with people who present 'difficult' or challenging behaviours. These sorts of behaviours are usually attributable to disagreement with decisions, feelings of injustice, anger or disappointment. The strength of these difficult behaviours or disagreements varies: moderate disagreements may imply some appreciation of others' views and there is the possibility of negotiations and compromise, whilst stronger reactions might range from rudeness, unprofessional behaviour and heated arguments to accusations and deceptions.

As a professional, you must learn to deal with these in a calm, productive way, drawing on communication strategies introduced earlier in this chapter. Active listening and helping the person/parties in conflict to clarify their own position and presenting alternative views clearly and calmly should help. There are some situations where you need to 'play for time' and be assertive in that you ask a person to wait until a later occasion or say 'Give me some time to think about what you are saying'. It is not productive or professional to become involved in trading insults or a shouting match, nor should you attempt to trivialise or 'laugh at' people who are clearly emotionally upset. You may find it easier to deal with parents and professionals from external services who present these behaviours than with colleagues from the same staff, because of the marked effect on working relationships. It is useful to develop a strategy for managing conflict.

Managing conflict:

1. *Confront the conflict* — admit to yourself that a conflict exists; inform the other party that there is a conflict; be firm about your views.
2. *Understand the other person's position* — listen; give feedback and restate their position to show you understand; use 'I' statements rather than 'you' and the language of blame.
3. *Clarify the problem(s)* — try and reach a mutual understanding; avoid aggression; recognise your strengths and weaknesses; be prepared to change if necessary; be honest.
4. *Search for and evaluate alternative solutions* — work together to find a mutually acceptable solution; create alternatives; evaluate them; deal with manageable problems first; ask yourself 'which solution looks best?' not 'which do I prefer?'
5. *Agree on and implement the best solution(s)* — treat the agreement like a contract; be clear; devise and write an action plan.
6. *Review progress* — have regular meetings to clarify objectives, to identify differences of opinion before they develop into conflict situations.

(Adapted from Keigh, 1988)

You might like to complete the following inventory, adapted from Everard and Morris (1990, pp. 107–8), to explore how you manage conflict:

Self-rating inventory

In the following self-rating inventory, think about any recent disagreements you have had at work, and rate yourself in terms of how you dealt with the situation on a scale of 1 (rarely) to 4 (frequently). In managing conflict do you:

1. Start by stating your beliefs and position?	1	2	3	4
2. Commence by asking whether you have made a mistake?	1	2	3	4
3. Avoid communicating with the other party?	1	2	3	4
4. Inform others about the situation?	1	2	3	4
5. Gain support from others?	1	2	3	4
6. Try to split the difference?	1	2	3	4
7. Try to justify your reason for raising the problem?	1	2	3	4
8. Listen carefully to the other point of view?	1	2	3	4
9. Adopt an aggressive manner?	1	2	3	4
10. Remain composed?	1	2	3	4
11. Try to understand the other viewpoint?	1	2	3	4
12. Try to pacify the other person?	1	2	3	4
13. Try to reach a quick solution?	1	2	3	4
14. Talk more than the other party?	1	2	3	4
15. Concentrate on potential solutions?	1	2	3	4
16. Reach agreement?	1	2	3	4
17. Give way to the other party?	1	2	3	4
18. Play down the scale of the problem?	1	2	3	4
19. Hope that the problem will go away?	1	2	3	4
20. Establish points on which there is agreement?	1	2	3	4
21. Attempt to win the conflict?	1	2	3	4
22. Immediately try to make amends?	1	2	3	4
23. Absolve yourself of any responsibility?	1	2	3	4
24. Try to solve the problem through negotiation and compromise?	1	2	3	4
25. Try to find a solution, which as far as possible, satisfies both parties?	1	2	3	4

To score the questionnaire place each of your results in the relevant section below:

Avoiding		Smoothing		Fighting		Compromising		Problem-solving	
Question	Score	Question	Score	Question	Score	Question	Score	Question	Score
3		2		1		6		8	
4		7		5		13		10	
17		12		9		16		11	
19		18		14		24		15	
23		22		21		25		20	
Total		Total		Total		Total		Total	

You should find that each of your highest scores indicates your preference for a particular response to a conflict situation. It may be appropriate to adopt these particular behaviours for different situations but in the light of your questionnaire results you might find that some of the behaviours you use are inappropriate for some of the conflict situations that you have experienced.

Avoiding

You avoid conflict by walking away and believe that life is easier by pretending the problem does not exist. It has a positive use in the short term because it does enable tempers to cool down. However, repeated use means that the cause of the conflict is never explored.

Smoothing

Your approach aims to help cool the situation down and may provide opportunities for objective consideration of the situation. It may also be appropriate if you are in the wrong or you wish to show others that you value their opinions. However, there are risks with this approach because you may be using it for fear that conflict might lead to you becoming less popular. People may lose respect for you because you appear to be unassertive and lacking in confidence.

Confrontation

You enjoy winning arguments and getting your own way even if this breeds resentment and hostility. However, in emergencies this approach is useful because you will act quickly and take decisions. It may also be required to implement unpopular actions or be used when you know that you are right when others are prevaricating. In the long term, repeated use of this strategy could result in low morale and poor problem solving because colleagues now believe that it is pointless raising issues with you even though they might have useful points to make.

Compromising

Your approach encourages quick solutions, which as far as possible, satisfy all parties. It can be useful when there is little time available to explore the issue in detail and the decision to be taken is not of major importance. Unfortunately

Verbal Skills for Managers

Rate yourself 1 (poor skills) to 5 (very effective) on the verbal skills listed below. Or ask a colleague (critical friend) to rate you — How well do I/am I...?

	Score
1. Listen actively to others	☐
2. Able and willing to negotiate	☐
3. Able to say 'no'	☐
4. Can cope with personal criticism	☐
5. Can present proposals/ideas	☐
6. Able to disagree without aggression	☐
7. Offer praise	☐
8. Can criticise constructively	☐
9. Contribute usefully to meetings	☐
10. Able to make a formal speech	☐
11. Argue logically	☐
12. Sound committed but not fanatical	☐
13. Summarise accurately what others say	☐
14. Avoid interrupting	☐
15. Chair meetings effectively	☐
16. Redefine problems as opportunities	☐
17. Obtain information (which others may wish to conceal)	☐
18. Question (without appearing inquisitorial)	☐
19. State even complicated issues clearly and simply	☐
20. Can handle differences of opinion	☐
Total score =	☐

A score below 84 suggests you must work hard to improve these skills

Adapted from Leigh, 1988

compromise solutions are not always of the highest quality because they rely on give-and-take at the expense of beliefs and merit.

Problem solving

Your aim is to get the parties to work together in order to find a solution which puts all concerned on the winning side. This involves a thorough examination of everyone's viewpoint and identifying an alternative course of action which maintains good working relationships. However, this approach is time consuming and may be used as an excuse to put off taking a decision.

In summary, to be an effective manager of conflict it is necessary to develop certain skills and attitudes. Develop your ability to manage conflict by considering the results of the questionnaire and look at the suitability of some of your recent responses to conflict and reflect upon whether you would deal with these differently, then practise and review whether your approach to conflict is changing.

Negotiating and persuading

Successful negotiation requires action which brings two or more opposing points of view together so that all are satisfied to an acceptable degree. Negotiation is not about one point of view winning over the others, but about creating a 'win/win' situation. Skilful negotiation requires you to understand the other person's position as well as your own and requires you to take a positive stance towards trying to think as the other person is thinking. Agreement is more likely to be reached if each party tries to see the other's perspective rather than responding immediately with a criticism, thus provoking further disagreement. It is important to keep calm and where possible let others talk first so that they feel they have 'had their say' before you start talking. Remember that an emotional outburst is not the start of the negotiation but an opportunity for an emotional release. While others are talking it is important to listen carefully and not use the time to rehearse your own argument in your head (effective listening). While others are talking, check for understanding so that when you are providing feedback the others appreciate that you are interested in their point of view. By doing this you are not only setting the tone for negotiation but also establishing a relationship which may lead to a more satisfactory outcome, i.e. acceptable agreement.

Analyse the interests which lie behind people's positions. The interests define the nature of the real problem as opposed to the stated position. As the interests are the reason for the decision, identifying them may help to find a solution or resolution. Arguing about the position will not be helpful. Agreement is always more likely if all groups reveal and explore their interests rather than state their positions. Successful negotiation is more likely to happen if this takes place.

It is important that you also are clear about your own position and interests. A skilled negotiator will be open about what they are thinking and feeling and will know their bottom line. In order to gain a win/win situation all groups must be able to see something for themselves in the final solution, negotiation is about acquiring something for all parties concerned. Sometimes it may be important to reach a compromise, even when you are disappointed in this, because someone has been prepared to shift their position. Thus if a colleague is 'prepared to trial' some new materials rather than say she will *adopt* them (which was your preference) and you can agree how their use will be evaluated, you may record this as a successful negotiation.

There will be many times when, as SENCO, you are trying to persuade colleagues to try new methods, change established practices or teach a child whose SEN are outside their experience. You will need to draw on all the skills outlined in this chapter. It is particularly important to share problems and possible solutions fully and honestly, and be able to give reasons. If colleagues (and parents) believe that you really are working to further children's interests rather than your own, then they are more open to your suggestions.

Summary

Managers require many verbal skills to facilitate effective communication:

- Listening actively without interrupting to encourage people to know that they have been heard and understood.
- Dealing with personal criticism and challenging the problems not the people.
- Being honest, thereby reducing suspicion about any hidden agendas.
- Using descriptive rather than evaluative language, to avoid people becoming too defensive.
- Providing specific feedback so that people communicate about actual facts rather than generalisations.
- Keeping composed so that situations do not become emotionally charged and tempers frayed.
- Negotiating to reach a solution.
- Offering praise and encouraging a sense of achievement.
- Stating proposals and issues in a clear and simple way.
- Making presentations.
- Chairing and contributing to meetings.

Chapter 4

Managing meetings and managing self

Garner (1996), reporting on the experiences of a small group of SENCOs, found that all of them said that their roles had changed considerably since 1993, from 'day-to-day teaching to a more managerial function'. They pointed particularly to their involvement in meetings — senior management meetings, case conferences/review meetings and liaison meetings with support service professionals.

Managing meetings

All meetings should be effectively organised and managed if they are to be purposeful and fulfil their aims and objectives and not waste time. Most meetings are costly in that they involve people giving valuable time to them.

For the purpose of this section consideration will be given to the management of meetings in general, more specific information concerning case conferences and reviews will be discussed in greater detail in a later chapter (see p. 87).

Preparing for a meeting

'Some people refer to meetings as a place where you take minutes and waste hours.' (Blanchard, Carew and Parisi-Carew, 1994, p. 44)

You should start by considering the *purpose* of the meeting and establishing its *objectives*. The agenda defines the purpose of the meeting, and should provide a working framework and

FIG 4.1
A bell curve model for timing
agenda items (Tropman, 1996)

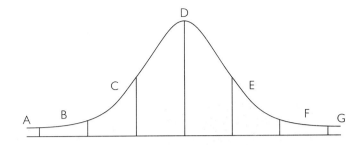

be more than just a list of items. How do you structure
your agenda? Do you use a 'typical agenda' of minutes,
matters arising, reports, old business, new business, and then
miscellaneous business? Do you consider such factors as time
so that you may provide for psychological and comfort needs,
and the attendance of key individuals?

Tropman (1996) recommends a bell curve model for timing
agenda items for meetings which plans for seven types of items
to be covered in a two-hour period. The seven items provide a
set of rules for framing effective and efficient meetings.
A. Introduce the agenda — relevant matters
B. Make informative announcements
C. Decide on less controversial items
D. Discuss the most difficult item
E. Break (if necessary)
F. Talk over items that are for discussion only
G. Consider the last item — adjourn if necessary.

Of course, two hours may be longer than most of the meetings
you hold, which will centre on reviews of children. However,
the important factor is to spend *most time* on the *most
important topic*!

Below are three checklists offering guidance on key aspects of
planning and managing effective meetings.

Checklist 1: Preparing for a meeting

1. Where and when should the meeting take place? What time
   will it start and finish? Is it formal or informal? (The seating
   arrangements can have an important effect on the effectiveness
   of the meeting.) Is confidentiality an issue? (This will affect the
   choice of venue).

2. A meeting should not last longer than two hours (one hour is preferable). If it is not possible to keep the meeting short, then make sure that proper 'comfort' breaks are provided.

3. Do you know (or can you find out) the opinions/views/needs, about a particular item, of those who will be attending the meeting?

4. Would it be useful to discuss specific issues with certain 'key personalities' in order to obtain some support, prior to the meeting?

5. In addition to sending out a written agenda, prepare your own agenda setting out some points for action or solutions. It may be advantageous to predict awkward questions and prepare reasoned answers. Does the meeting require participants to have read certain documentation? If so, make sure that supporting paperwork is sent out with the agenda.

6. Circulate the information in good time, providing both a starting and expected finishing time.

7. Is it necessary (or would it be advisable?) to send 'courtesy' copies to those who will not be attending the meeting but might have an interest in the proceedings?

8. If undesirable or unsatisfactory outcomes start to emerge during the meeting, what will you do? Anticipate these and make contingency plans!

9. Are all the people attending the meeting familiar with the formality of meetings and the possible power relationships that might arise? How are people who may be at some disadvantage in respect of experience of such meetings, to be prepared/helped?

10. Will all those attending be acquainted with the nature of the language and jargon used? If not, how might they be prepared, or how will the language be adjusted?

Checklist 2: Chairing the meeting

1. Start on time.

2. Introduce/welcome individuals, particularly those who have not attended before. Ensure that everybody is aware of who is present (names, roles and reasons for presence). Consider the use of name cards.

3. Ensure that interruptions are not allowed to intrude upon the meeting, unless in an emergency.

4. Introduce each agenda item.

5. Encourage contributions. How effectively, in the time available, can you motivate all participants to ensure that they make a full contribution to the discussion and utilise their individual expertise/viewpoints?

6. Take clear control. Deal with contributions in a polite manner. Maintain the momentum of the meeting, keeping an eye on the time. You need to be able to do this discreetly. You may need to impose time limits on the discussion of each item to avoid spending too much time on trivia as well as keeping to the proposed finishing time for the meeting. However, when you are discussing issues affecting a child's future, you should bear in mind the child's *needs* are more important than running a meeting on time, and agree to adjourn if necessary.

7. Be aware of 'hidden agendas'. These may be anything that may influence behaviour or prejudice decision making. They are 'hidden' because most people will be ignorant of them, and they are 'agendas' in the sense that they are the intentions of certain participants who wish to influence the meeting in a particular way.

8. Keep a balance between the aims/task and the needs of the individuals participating in the meeting. Maintain harmonious relationships.

9. Listen carefully! Invite silent members to participate and welcome their contributions. Take decisions. Summarise key points and try to cut through waffle. Record decisions and points for actions, including by whom and by when. Ensure a plan for implementing actions is put in place. Help the person taking minutes. Keep checking on the understanding of participants (this helps clarify the situation).

10. Conclude the meeting on time and if a further meeting is required then arrange while all are still present.

Checklist 3: Taking and using minutes

A minute is a record of what the meeting discussed and decided about a particular agenda item. The following are the points that should be included in the minutes:

1. All decisions reached by the meeting and any agreements made not to make a decision or act upon something.

2. Any action required in order to implement a decision.

3. A record of who will take the action.

4. Time limits or deadlines for the action.

5. If the meeting is formal then the minutes should also include: the full text of any motion or resolution; names of proposers and seconders; and the result of the vote as announced by the person chairing the meeting.

6. The minute-taker should know how much information to include concerning: background details; discussion; whether points should be recorded in detail or summarised; and whether to attribute comments to named individuals.

7. The minutes should record important points made leading to decisions, record the decisions, and the action required to implement the decision. Each minute should be self-contained.

8. Minutes should be impartial and factual and should not include emotional remarks made by individuals or judgmental words. Initials, first names only and 'jargon' should not be used unless it is certain that everyone using the minutes will understand them and there is no possibility of confusion.

9. If a consistent format is used it will be easier to follow the progression of related meetings.

10. Numbering the minutes makes it easier to refer back to them. Such systems might include a standardised numbering system for agenda and minutes, and using the same numbers all the time even if there is nothing to record a particular numbered item on some occasions.

How effective are your meetings?

A valuable way of improving the effectiveness of meetings is by evaluating them. Honey (1988) captures the difference between ineffective and effective meetings in Figure 4.2.

Improving the quality of your meetings

You can evaluate the quality of your meetings by observing and recording meetings and then sharing the outcomes with participants. When observing a meeting it is essential that a distinction is made between content and process. Content is about how the members of the meeting are achieving its aims and objectives, process is about the way in which the meeting goes about achieving the task. An example of a checklist for observing and evaluating the effectiveness of a meeting is given below. Try to observe a meeting which you do not chair in order to heighten your awareness of the value of 'good meetings'.

Characteristics of an ineffective meeting	Characteristics of an effective meeting
Size Over 12 participants	About 7 participants as long as they all have something to contribute
Frequency Daily (because familiarity breeds contempt)	Preferably once a week if it is for the same group of participants. This makes a meeting sufficiently 'special' to keep people on their toes
Duration Over 2 hours	An hour but 2 hours should be an absolute maximum. If not possible because people have come from different locations ensure proper breaks after each hour period
Objectives Objectives are non-existent and/or they are implied and vague	Objectives are clear, explicitly agreed and challenging
Agenda The agenda is non-existent or only in the mind of the Chair and not shared with participants.	Either there is a written agenda 48 hours in advance of meetings or the meeting starts with communal agenda setting
Skills of the Chair No control, structure or summaries; makes all decisions; does all talking	Looks after process, orchestrates discussion, summarises to check understanding and agreement of actions
Participation Some people say a lot; others say nothing	People contribute in open, virtually enthusiastic way
Problem Solving Problems identified but not addressed. People jump to conclusions about causes/solutions and do not consider pros and cons of alternatives	Systematic approach i.e. specify problem, collect information, generate ideas, evaluate alternatives, agree best course of action, planning and implementation
Interruptions Messages etc. allowed to intrude meeting, people wander in and out to deal with things that are happening outside meeting	No interruptions
Conclusions Vague or non-existent	Specific conclusions/actions summarised and noted so that everyone knows exactly who is supposed to do what as a consequence of the meeting

(Adapted from Honey, *Improve your people skills* 1988, pp. 108–9)

FIG 4.2
Characteristics of ineffective and effective meetings

Observing a meeting

1. *Management of meeting*

   Is there a lively exchange of views and ideas with each person regulating their individual contribution and the discussion pleasant and harmonious?

   Are one or two participants taking control over the topic(s) raised?

   Is the chairperson keeping the meeting on task and encouraging contributions from all participants?

   Is the discussion going round in circles?

   Is time being wasted by the discussion of irrelevancies and trivia?

   Is the Chair summarising points and making recommendations?

   Are participants arguing and discussion taking place on a 'win/lose' basis?

2. *Decision making*

   Are decisions ideas based on a full understanding and agreement/Are the majority in agreement?

   Are decisions based on a compromise solution?

   Are all views/ideas dealt with or are some lost within the discussion?

   Do any participants use a power/status position to dominate the decision-making process?

   Are ideas/views supported by a few individuals, a course of action taken?

   Are participants concerned to agree and maintain harmony?

3. *Discussion*

   Are participants friendly towards each other and being polite allowing 'give' and 'take'?

   Are some individuals concerned more with personal victory than accepting the best solution?

   Are points of disagreement identified and dealt with in an open and honest way?

   Do those with differing opinions/ideas reach acceptable positions and change stance in order to move progress?

   Are all participants involved in the discussion?

4. *Atmosphere of the meeting*

   Do all participants appear to find the meeting interesting and useful?

   Is the meeting fairly 'laid back' and pleasant?

   Are individuals competitive and critical?

   Does the meeting seem to have very little purpose?

   Do individuals appear to be motivated, challenging and committed to the task?

5. *Aims of the meeting*

   Are the aims of the meeting fully appreciated by all and are all participants working towards fulfilling the aim?

As so much time may be taken up by meetings, it is worth spending time to discover how to make them more efficient. It is also worth deciding whether there are *more* meetings than necessary. If the business of a meeting could be conducted in another way (such as a briefing meeting) then use alternative forms of communication. However, where a central aim is to foster inclusion, participation and empowerment (as at decision-making staff meetings and case conferences) then a paper exercise is not a satisfactory substitute.

Time management

Many SENCOs, particularly in primary schools, feel there is so much paperwork and other activities to do, in addition to their teaching role, that they 'never have enough time' to complete administrative tasks to their satisfaction. Indeed, OFSTED (1996) reports that many SENCOs only accomplish the requirements of their role by using time in the evenings and at weekends. Many other teachers would suggest that this is not unique to SENCOs and that lesson preparation, marking, report writing and professional updating are regular 'out-of-school' activities. There is no doubt that effective use of time is an important management skill. It is extremely difficult to balance teaching commitments, organisational and administrative activities including the amount of paperwork required for annual reviews and planning meetings. Although little can be done to alleviate individual situations regarding workload, it may be useful to think about some procedures and instruments which might help you reappraise the organisation of your time.

A good start is to look at time-wasters which are relevant to you, and possible solutions (see Figure 4.3).

You can see from Figure 4.3 that time management is a personal process which relies upon self-discipline in both setting personal and professional goals and priorities and then planning and implementing them. Depending upon your self-management style you may not at first be able to forecast how much time certain tasks and activities take. So having considered your goals it is then useful to analyse how you spend your time over a period of a few weeks. This may be

Problem	Action
Trying to do too much	<ul><li>learn to say no</li><li>devise a system, e.g. daily/weekly planner</li></ul>
No time to develop a plan	<ul><li>set time aside, say 1 hour each week; set priorities</li></ul>
Unclear objectives, priorities and planning	<ul><li>use the planning time to clarify your objectives</li></ul>
Procrastination (putting off doing a disliked or difficult task)	<ul><li>decide to tackle tasks in order of priority and timescale</li></ul>
Too much paperwork	<ul><li>sort through all your proforma and records and try to reduce in number or complexity</li><li>deal with paperwork as it comes in on a daily basis (file or bin as appropriate)</li><li>delegate where appropriate</li></ul>
Disorganised desk or office	<ul><li>delegate some time to clearing the 'clutter'. Very often this is a pile of papers we thought 'couldn't be thrown away'</li><li>deal with these by filing or discarding</li><li>when it is clear, ask for any incoming mail or notes to be left in a simple 'in-tray'</li><li>deal with paperwork daily</li><li>make considered decisions about what paper to retain</li><li>organise the space and your files so that under your new 'planned day' you can maintain them</li></ul>
Crisis management	<ul><li>minimise the chances for crises by planning ahead</li><li>delegate some activities</li><li>say 'no' to some situations where you are not the only person who could deal with the crisis</li></ul>
Attending ineffective meetings	<ul><li>plan more effectively (as in this chapter)</li></ul>
Lacking specific skills or knowledge to manage a situation	<ul><li>plan your own professional development, including finding time to read (rather than worrying about what you don't know)</li><li>use the SENCO forum</li></ul>
Frequent interruptions	<ul><li>make it known when you are using an 'open-door' policy</li><li>use an appointments system</li><li>agree that at certain times you will have a 'please do not disturb sign' on the door</li></ul>
Staff seek advice frequently, informally, and you want to be seen to be supportive	<ul><li>deal with as 'interruptions'</li><li>agree to call an end to a meeting and arrange another time to meet</li><li>identify areas for staff development</li></ul>
Time spent 'chasing up' staff for reports on children	<ul><li>send a memo with a deadline</li><li>agree to a time for a meeting (some would prefer this to writing replies)</li></ul>

FIG 4.3
Tips for tackling time-wasters

done by keeping a log which details exactly how you spend your time including such activities as:

- teaching
- administration
- attendance at meetings
- marking
- talking to colleagues
- telephone conversations
- seeing parents
- meeting external support
- breaks

At the end of the period the knowledge gained should prove extremely valuable for future planning. You should be able to predict the time some of the identified tasks and activities usually take without over- or under-estimating them. You might also generate some ideas for making changes to increase efficiency. Alongside this it is necessary to use other methods of controlling your time such as an action diary and project planning.

An action diary is commonly used by managers and is simply a method of writing down dates for meetings and appointments; deadlines by when tasks need to be completed; and allocating time for preparing, planning and marking. This should be kept by your side so that you may write these down as they occur. Ensure that you check your diary regularly. Each time that you find you have not accomplished a task, analyse the reason. If the task still has to be done, re-set your priorities. Make adjustments to the nature of the task or timescale where appropriate. Check on the extent to which your tasks are relying on others rather than yourself when you seek explanations about non-completion.

Daily agenda/planner

Many people plan a daily agenda and it is worth considering this as it takes only a few minutes to plan.

First block in your teaching contract time
Then
List the items to do
Number them in terms of priority

Estimate the time each will take

Check to see if any can be delegated to a colleague, support assistant, secretary, welfare officer, visiting teacher, parent or pupil

Write 'D' beside any such task and indicate a deadline given to the delegate

Re-number your tasks in order of priority

Review at the end of the day or start of next day.

Project planning

Project planning involves thinking through a project and drawing up an action plan which includes details of the project, providing information about it for all those that will need to know, and setting 'do by' dates and slots for doing the project.

Reviewing your objectives and role

Good time management is not the same as 'saving' time — it is using our time effectively to achieve our goals. It is, therefore, vital that if you decide to use an action diary/planner, you must be clear about how you determine your priorities and tasks. In order to do this you must bear in mind your goals and responsibilities as a SENCO *and* as a class teacher. This is where having a job description, and having undertaken the activities proposed in the first chapter, will help you to be clear about your overall aims and priorities. Planning your time means you will work more *efficiently* not *more*. Two key areas we have mentioned above are worth further elaboration:

- delegating and
- learning how to say 'no'.

These are often particularly difficult skills for SENCOs to acquire, largely because of certain perceptions:

- A SENCO must be able to support colleagues, children, parents (and by extension everyone).
- It is essential for a SENCO to be 'approachable' and if you refuse to take on a task, you may appear less so in future.
- Very often the record-keeping and curriculum differentiation which is necessary to meet children's SEN is already viewed as an 'additional burden' by many teachers,

and a SENCO is reluctant to do anything which might provoke further negative attitudes.

Moreover, in many small primary schools, all teachers may be 'middle managers' or subject coordinators (some for several subjects) all seeking to delegate.

Delegation

Often it is tempting to do everything yourself either because it seems quicker, or for fear that someone might do it better or you feel that you can do it better than anyone else. Most importantly, in the context of managing time, delegation provides opportunities for saving some of your own time to spend on tasks that only you can do. We appreciate that as a coordinator there may be relatively few opportunities to delegate. However, by considering the simple questions in the suggested activity you may find that you are unwilling to delegate due to your insecurity rather than a reasoned judgment about who might be the best person to do the job.

It is important also to consider the nature of a task which can be delegated and to think of the most appropriate people to do it — not necessarily your teaching colleagues. Make a list of some of the tasks you do routinely and then consider whether anyone else (including pupils and/or parents) could do them.

Another facet of failure to delegate to colleagues is the effect it can have on those who may feel you have no confidence in their abilities or those who, as junior members of staff, would like to learn more about the role of SENCO and wish to further their career in this way. Above all, 'doing everything yourself' as a SENCO is not only an inefficient use of time, it also serves to 'mystify' special educational needs and do very little to implement inclusive approaches in your school.

Learning to say 'no'

Some of the principles discussed under 'delegation' underpin our reasons for finding it difficult to refuse to accept every task that we are asked to take on. What is important is to:

- *Decide* whether or not this is a task you want to do.
- Say *no* if you — do not want to do it and it is not
    essentially part of your remit;

Suggestion

Attitudes to delegation

Consider the following questions concerning delegation and share your responses and feelings with a colleague.

a) Do you ever feel that you do more work than other colleagues? If 'yes', have you thought about why you do more work?

b) Are there aspects of your job that you enjoy doing and would not wish to give up?

c) Do you believe that you are indispensable? Why?

d) How do you ask other people to do tasks?

e) When you do delegate do you monitor progress? How?

f) Do you trust your colleagues. If not, why not?

g) Do you provide feedback and praise?

h) Do you envy colleagues who are successful?

i) Do you try to do everything yourself?

> It is our experience that when people are seen to be hard-working and efficient, no-one is offended to have a request which implies further work, turned down.

— think someone else is more appropriate;
— give reasons (not excuses) and suggest *other solutions*.

If you do not learn to say no then not only do you *add* to your workload, but you may spend more time doing work which is the responsibility of someone else at the expense of discharging your own responsibilities. You may fail to complete *any* task effectively by trying to tackle too many. It is also worth remembering that if you are always prepared to take on additional work, it is difficult to convince colleagues that a SENCO has a demanding role!

Apply time management techniques in both your working and personal life and be firm with both friends at home and colleagues at work. Wherever possible organise work in blocks to aid concentration. Plan your administrative work so that you do not get too much on one particular day or week and when at home decide at which time of the day you work best. Organise highly demanding jobs at your peak time, i.e. when you feel you are at your freshest. Always keep writing materials at hand — how often do you spend time hunting for a pen or pencil? Find a balance between rushing a job and being too methodical. Finally make sure that you make the most of your leisure time — try not to take work on holiday with you — because a major benefit of effective time management is the restoration of leisure time.

Most managers would say that effective time management is a major form of stress management. By achieving targets and goals, and by planning work in small, manageable tasks, you begin to feel in 'control' of your own life. The main source of stress is when you feel you have 'lost control' and can see no means of recovery.

Managing Stress

Garner (1996), Lewis (1996) and Bowers (1996) all suggest that the administrative load associated with the Code of Practice is a major source of stress for many SENCOs, largely because there is insufficient time built in to timetabling arrangements in schools. This is particularly true in primary schools. Although we are here addressing stress as a negative state, Everard and Morris (1996) suggest that some amount of stress may be valuable:

> ❝ *It provides challenge and motivation, helps raise performance and is an ingredient of job satisfaction. Lack of stimulation such as stress can lead to boredom which paradoxically is itself stressful.*
> (Everard and Morris, 1996, p. 114)

However, stress can become overwhelming and then it has a deleterious effect on people's ability to function. Very often, as a SENCO, you have to try to manage not only your own stress, but that of others, so it is worth considering how to identify stress 'signals'.

Signs of Stress

Physiological/Health	*Emotional*	*Behavioural*
■ increased heart rate	■ anxiety, fear	■ outbursts of anger
■ headaches, backaches	■ depression	■ crying
■ stomach upsets	■ apathy	■ increased smoking, drinking, drug-taking
■ low energy levels	■ anger/tantrums	■ avoiding work
■ indigestion	■ irritability	■ decrease in work rate
	■ feelings of inadequacy	■ accident-prone
	■ low self-esteem	■ unable to concentrate
		■ unpredictable
		■ over-eating ('bingeing'.)

Dunham (1994) outlines two main approaches to managing stress:
1. Identify the factors within a situation (or the person's perception of those factors) which are proving to be stressful and try to alter them.
2. Develop strategies for coping with the physiological, emotional, cognitive and behavioural reactions to stress.

An example of the first of these approaches would be if you identified that you feel 'trapped' between trying to meet your headteacher's expectations of you in managing SEN provision in the school and working with colleagues who do not see this as a priority. Some of the ways of dealing with this would include:

- talking openly to the headteacher and colleagues and trying to persuade colleagues of the significance of your role;
- asking the head to clarify your role on paper and to the staff;
- setting some short-term, achievable targets for yourself in relation to your role.

Examples of the second approach include the development of personal strategies to help you deal with stress symptoms and maintain control at difficult times. Moss (1995) believes that it is important for you as SENCO to consider your own needs, find time to *think* about your practice and *talk* to somebody about how things are going.

Stress-busters	
REASONING	Self-talk, e.g. 'I have been through this sort of thing before,' 'I know I can cope,' 'Last year I did "x" and that was far more demanding,' etc.
PRIORITISE	As in time management, plan your time more effectively to give some time to other activities.
HUMOUR	Reduce tension by telling jokes or watching TV/films which are 'light comedy'.
RELAX	Use relaxation exercises; do some breathing exercises; make yourself a drink and sit down with it *without* work beside you; have 30 minutes 'R and R' on reaching home (Rest and Recuperation!).
READ	Magazines, novels, travel books or brochures (anything not work-related).
EXERCISE	Walk or run during lunch hour — even if only to some local shops or post office.
REFOCUS	Think of someone else's situation; visualise your holiday ahead, etc.
TIME MANAGEMENT	See earlier section — this is the best stress-buster for most people.
EAT REGULARLY	Think how often you are not having breakfast or a lunch; are you snacking? Stress often affects eating habits.

Suggestion

Answer some of the following questions and share answers with a colleague:
a) In your personal and social life do you talk about issues that are unrelated to your work?
b) Do you set aside a specific amount of time for talking about work at home and then discuss other topics?
c) Do you take an interest in other activities other than work?
d) Do you enjoy being involved in trivial things such as mowing the lawn or taking the dog for a walk?
e) Do you exercise to 'burn' off tension?
f) Do you make sure that you have time for your hobbies and favourite pastimes?

Negative responses to the majority of these questions suggests that you should consider making some improvements to your personal and social life and consider the benefits you will gain.

It is also worth trying to keep a 'balance' in your life, and to try to prevent stress generated at work from pervading your personal life (and vice versa).

As one of the managers of a school, however, you should also consider how you can influence stress management (and prevention) at an organisational level, for it is not sufficient to believe that coping with stress should be seen only as an individual's responsibility.

How schools as organisations may reduce stress

- clear job descriptions
- clear management structure
- a realistic school development plan
- planned continuing professional development to meet a school's expectations and personal needs
- provide a suitable physical environment (noise levels, ventilation, etc.)
- provide adequate teaching and learning resources
- involve staff in decision making
- make maximum, planned use of non-teaching staff
- develop and maintain good relationships with parents
- a senior management team which acknowledges and praises teachers' efforts
- encourage teachers to work as teams who provide mutual support

Above all, do not feel obliged to enter and magnify a 'stress culture' where you begin to feel guilty if you are not saying you are 'under stress'. Good management skills and job satisfaction put you in control of your own life.

Chapter 5

Managing the SEN policy, practices and procedures under the Code of Practice

A major responsibility of the SEN Co-ordinator is for 'the day-to-day operation of the school's SEN policy' (DFE, 1994a, p. 9). The crucial questions for you to address, as coordinator, are:

■ Does the school's policy 'have regard to' the Code of Practice?

■ Are the school's practices in line with its policy?

It is important to evaluate your current SEN policy and make amendments where necessary. You might begin by looking at the recommendations for a school SEN policy in the Code of Practice. It is important, however, not to produce a 'sterile' policy: your school's policy should reflect the philosophy, context and needs of its staff and pupils. In consultation with colleagues, the headteacher and SEN governor (and drawing on parental consultation) you should consider whether there is an aspect of *your* school's approach to SEN which is not mentioned in the Code, but which your school wishes to include. An example of this might be recognition of the needs of very able and gifted pupils. Many mainstream schools include this group within their SEN policy, whilst acknowledging such pupils do not have SEN under the definitions of the Education Act (unless, of course, they experience considerable learning or behavioural difficulties or physical/sensory impairment). Some schools may wish to include a reference to the provision they make for supporting children who might 'miss' a period of schooling, whether for a short or long time whatever the reason for absence. Using the guidelines from the Code and your school's own additions, you will be in a position to evaluate your school's policy and practices.

We are assuming, in this book, that your school already has a policy and that all (or most) of the staff have been involved in developing it. It is important that governors too, have been involved. Staff are only likely to implement the policy, however, if they believe that the practices required are *manageable* as part of their teaching responsibilities, and that they will be supported by you or others where appropriate. The policy should make lines of responsibility clear, and, as stated in Chapter 1, your role and relationships to staff and the SEN procedures should be written down and understood by colleagues, parents and governors. In many cases there is also a need for you to liaise with the school's professional development coordinator in order to identify staff development needs and ways of meeting these. This aspect is pursued in Chapter 13.

It is important that staff know how to implement the policy at all stages of the process and are fully aware of pertinent legislation. They should also be aware of the fact that an OFSTED inspection will include an evaluation of their practices in relation to the school's SEN policy.

Reviewing the school's SEN policy

The 1993 Education Act requires that:

❝ *The annual report for each school shall include a report containing such information as may be prescribed about the implementation of the governing body's policy for pupils with special educational needs.* (Education Act, 1993, Section 161, 5)

You therefore need to keep your policy and practices under review if you are to be able to report fully to the governing body, whose annual report must include information on the following, as required in the Education (SEN) (Information) Regulations, Regulation 5 and Schedule 4 (Statutory Instruments, 1994):

- the success of the SEN policy;
- significant changes in the policy;
- any consultation with the LEA, the funding authority and other schools;
- how resources have been allocated to and amongst children with special educational needs over the year.

Clearly, information on the last two areas mentioned above will be drawn from your record system, but the first two imply you have undertaken an evaluation.

> We suggest your review should have three major aspects:
> 1. *Does the policy meet the recommendations of the Code of Practice?*
> 2. *Is there a match between policy and practices?*
>   Do staff understand how to operate the policy? (Are there appropriate structures in place?)
> 3. *Is the policy/practice effective?*
>   (Are the pupils' SEN being identified and met appropriately?)

The last question is more difficult to answer, but, as suggested earlier, the first two questions might be evaluated by drawing up a checklist of policy items and identifying the related practices. You can use this review, however, as an opportunity for staff development by undertaking an activity such as that above, where you invite colleagues to identify and discuss the school's procedures and say how their personal practices implement the policy. This activity should ensure they feel 'continuing ownership' of the policy, further develop their understanding, and highlight areas of concern or difficulty. You might, therefore, use a staff meeting or staff development session to ask them to complete and discuss the checklist below. They could be invited to complete the form individually, prior to the session, and come prepared to discuss their comments. What is important is to involve them, at some stage, in discussion.

Of course, you can use the checklist for your own personal review if you prefer. This activity for Reviewing a School's Policy for SEN (Figure 5.1) is taken from one of the inservice activities in Phillips and Cockett's (1995) INSET package *SEN: Putting the Code to Work*.

Area Addressed	In written policy	Clarity	Accuracy	Compre-hensiveness	Sense of audience	Practices in place	Priority for action
1. The principles/philosophy on which policy/practices are based							
2. Definitions of Special Educational Needs							
3. The name of the SEN Coordinator							
4. The roles and responsibilities of headteacher, coordinator and governors in relation to SEN							
5. Arrangements for coordinating provision for pupils with SEN							
6. Arrangements for admissions provision for pupils with SEN							
7. Information about SEN specialism(s) at the school, or special unit							
8. Details of any special facilities which increase or assist access to the school for those with SEN							
9. Arrangements for identification and assessment of SEN							
10. A clear, staged procedure showing what the classteacher, coordinator and headteacher do before seeking external help/support							
11. Availability of special resources, materials and learning support within the school							
12. Clear process and procedures for monitoring, recording and reviewing progress							
13. Arrangements for providing access for pupils with SEN to a balanced and broadly based curriculum, including the National Curriculum; arrangements for differentiation							
14. Arrangements for integrating pupils with SEN within the school as a whole							

Area Addressed	In written policy	Clarity	Accuracy	Compre-hensiveness	Sense of audience	Practices in place	Priority for action
15. Criteria and arrangements for monitoring and evaluating the success of the school's SEN policy							
16. Arrangements for considering complaints about the SEN provision in the school							
17. Staff development opportunities for inservice related to SEN							
18. Use made of teachers and facilities from outside the school including support services							
19. Arrangements for partnerships with parents							
20. Links with other mainstream schools and special schools							
21. Links as above, with particular reference to arrangements when pupils change schools or leave school							
22. Links with health and social services and any voluntary organisation							
23. Liaison with educational support services e.g. educational psychologists, learning support services, educational welfare etc.							
24, 25 and 26 are not directly stated within the Code, but may be found useful.							
24. Relevant policies explained to all parents before children are entered on the school roll							
25. Specific additional arrangements (if any) for pupils with statements							
26. Arrangements for pupils who are absent from school for: a) short } periods b) extended } of time							

© The Manchester Metropolitan University. Didsbury School of Education.

From: *Special Educational Needs: Putting the Code to Work*

FIG 5.1a
Reviewing the school's policy for SEN

FIG 5.1b
Criteria for evaluating the documentation

1. Consider the written policy first, placing a tick in the first column if the area is mentioned in the policy.
2. Then consider what the policy says, evaluating it using the criteria below.
   Clarity
   Is the information described clearly?
   Is it easy to understand?
   Accuracy
   Is the information valid and reliable? (Does it describe what really exists?)
   Comprehensiveness
   Is there sufficient information and detail?
   Sense of Audience
   Can the language be easily understood by teachers, support services personnel (who may only visit occasionally), parents and governors?
   Is the information useful to teachers, other professionals and parents?

Suggestion

Reviewing the School's Policy and Practices for SEN

1. Photocopy on to 2 sides of A4 paper the review schedule (Figure 5.1a) and supply each member of staff with a copy and a copy of the Criteria for Evaluating the Documentation (Figure 5.1b).
2. Ask staff to work in pairs and to use the criteria to evaluate the school's policy by completing the first five columns. (This will take 15–20 minutes or can be done individually prior to the meeting.)
3. Ask for feedback as to where there might be a need to revise the policy.
4. Ask them to indicate in column 6, following discussion in pairs, where they can agree as to the relevant practices and procedures already in place, leaving blank any cell where they are uncertain or unable to identify practices. (This will take about 15 minutes)
5. Lead a group discussion about any perceived needs for clarifying, implementing or modifying practices.
6. Devise an Action Plan setting objectives and review dates.

Your role in this activity is to act as a facilitator and note any areas where there is misunderstanding or difficulty, in order to adjust the practices, or identify a need for staff development. You need to take some (or total) responsibility for devising the plan which addresses the outcomes.

Evaluating effectiveness: Is the policy successful?

Evaluating *effectiveness* will be more difficult.
- What criteria will be used?
- Who will be involved in the evaluation?

In establishing criteria you must revisit the policy and its objectives, which will have been particularly concerned with:
- identifying and assessing SEN;
- providing access to the primary curriculum;
- making appropriate provision for pupils to make progress;
- reviewing pupils' progress and raising achievement;
- use of outside services and agencies.

You need to consider what performance indicators were set, or establish them now. You might, therefore:

- examine the timetables of some of the children with SEN to investigate *how* they spend their time;
- carry out observations of these children to see if they are engaged in learning activities in a range of lessons;
- examine IEPs and 'review' information to discover what progress pupils have made including SATs information;
- investigate the ways in which outside support has been a factor in the progress of pupils, distinguishing between the support given by parents from that of professionals;
- examine the school's curriculum documents to see how these address SEN;
- observe and account for the extent to which children with statements are integrated into mainstream classes (proportion of time).

You should consider how governors, teachers, parents and pupils might also be engaged in an evaluation process. You could use the questionnaire below for *all* groups, although it was devised for use with teachers and L.S.As.

Involving staff

You might collect information through a general discussion or use a questionnaire method such as the example below.

Questionnaire for teachers/classroom or learning support assistants

1. Do you feel you understand the school's SEN policy and its related practices?   YES/NO
   Please identify any aspects requiring further clarification and improvement.
2. Do you have enough information about children with SEN in your class
   - with statements?   YES/NO
   - on the SEN Register but not at Stage 5?   YES/NO
   If the answer is No, please say what further information you would like.
3. What further information would you like about:
   - my role as coordinator and availability for support?
   - availability of support from external services?

- appropriate teaching methods?
- access to knowledge of special materials and resources?

4. Are there any areas related to SEN where you would wish to have further professional development? How might this be facilitated?

Using pupils' views

You might talk to children with SEN, using the following sort of questions. (We suggest you present these in an informal, supportive way, not as listed below as that could suggest a formal interrogation. The language used should be adjusted to the child's level.)

- What do you like doing in school? What makes you happy in school?
- What sort of things in school are you good at? What do you think you're not so good at?
- Would you like (do you get) any help with some things? What could help you to do better?
- What sort of things would you really like to be good at
  — in school?
  — out of school?
- If you could change school and the way teachers (we) help you do things or to learn really well, what would you change?

Finding out parents' views

Use meetings (or any contact) with parents of pupils with SEN to find out their opinions as to how far they feel:

- they have been fully *informed* about their child's needs, the provision made and progress;
- they have been *involved* in planning the individual education plan;
- the school could do more to involve them;
- their opinions have been *valued*;
- the school has been *successful* in meeting their child's needs (and what more it could do).

Again you could use a questionnaire format if you preferred, but you need to be aware (a) that you may get a very low response, (b) not all parents may be able to read, (c) of the home language of the parents.

> Any decisions to make amendments to the school's policy should involve all staff.

Reporting on the policy

It is your responsibility to collect information and prepare a report for governors, the senior management team and/or colleagues. Where you discover an area of weakness, there should be an action plan to show how a new or modified practice will be established and monitored. You can, of course, use the items in the policy as a checklist. It is important to identify those parts of the policy which operate well, in addition to acknowledging any problematic area. An example of the latter, in our experience, is that teachers are vexed by the issue over the first step in *registering a concern*: how do they make a decision that a child may have SEN?

Writing reports

There are several key points to observe when writing effective reports, which can be applied to other occasions.

Who is the report for?

Who requested it and why? Will anybody else be reading it? Even though you may be directing the report to a team of people, think of a key person and keep that person in mind when writing the report. What do they want to know?

How long should the report be?

It is important to hold a reader's interest and, therefore, ensure that it is not a lengthy document with far too many points. Make a list of the key points that you need to make and ensure that you keep to these points. Read through the report and remove unnecessary information.

Is the report comprehensible?

Will the audience *understand* your report? Use short sentences, make paragraphs concise, avoid the use of jargon and always proof read it carefully.

Does your report have a structure?

There are a variety of structures which may be used for writing reports. An example might be:

- an executive summary (usually no longer than 2 sides), to provide an overview of what the report set out to do and its conclusions;

- the main report including title, index, introduction analysis of information, conclusions and recommendations;
- supporting material which may be placed in appendices.

It is usual for reports to be presented on single-sided paper (only in the case of lengthy reports may it be advisable to use both sides). Signal what each section is about by using headings or use separate sheets of paper. Ensure that there is a logical flow to your writing and that the reader is clear about the structure. A list of contents helps the reader to understand the sequence.

Is the report presented well?

Has it been checked for typographical errors, correct punctuation, spelling mistakes and correct numbering? Does the title page create interest? Is the layout reader-friendly, i.e. is there a need for double-spacing? Does the binding enable the reader to turn the pages with ease? Is the numbering system consistent? Are all diagrams, graphs and charts properly labelled?

Is the report accountable?

Does the report provide conclusions, recommendations or suggestions? It is assumed that you know more about the subject than the person(s) who has asked for the report, so you should always take responsibility for interpreting the information rather than just presenting facts. Will you be available to answer any questions which arise from it?

Managing procedures

The Code of Practice proposes a model on which schools can base their procedures for identifying and meeting SEN. As SENCO you have responsibility for organising these procedures, managing the record-keeping systems for pupils with SEN, organising reviews and case conferences. Many SENCOs (and their colleagues) have become concerned at the proliferation of paperwork, and, in many cases, responsibility for some of the record-keeping has been devolved to class teachers, and the management of annual reviews of children with statements has been assumed by the headteacher. In most schools, however, the SENCO is responsible for the following tasks:

Stages 1–5 — monitoring and reviewing the school's policy;
— maintaining the school's SEN Register;
— liaising with class teachers in devising, developing and reviewing IEPs.

Stages 2–3 — organising any special support from within the school's own resources or calling on external agencies.

Stage 4 — organising the paperwork and preparing an assessment report to support a request for multi-disciplinary assessment at Stage 4.

Stages 4–5 — contributing an assessment report/school's evidence towards Appendix D of statutory assessment.

Stage 5 — developing IEPs for children with statements;
— monitoring and reviewing each IEP (on a termly or half-termly basis, or at least twice a year);
— organising the annual reviews of children with statements.

The SENCO may, additionally, be asked to prepare material for SEN tribunals, and, indeed, may be called upon as a 'witness' by either the parents or the LEA (or both!). If record-keeping is well maintained and you have a good understanding of how your school is *financed* and *supported by LEA services*, then this aspect should *not* involve extra work. Nevertheless, we have included a short section on preparation for tribunals later in this chapter (see p. 95).

Clarity about your procedures and evidence that the SEN policy is operating successfully are also essential for OFSTED inspections (as mentioned in Chapter 13). It is important not to let 'OFSTED' drive your procedures, but it may well be useful to consider how to be prepared for an inspection. As with preparation for a tribunal, if your systems are in place, then notification of an impending inspection should not imply 'extra' or 'new' work.

Managing the paperwork and records

It is important, of course, to keep good, reliable records relating to the acknowledgment of a child's SEN (the SEN Register), the assessment reports for the child, Individual Education Plans

(IEPs), records monitoring progress, and review and case conference reports. Most schools have now devised a set of proformas, and in some cases LEAs have provided models, or requested the use of standard forms which will ease collaboration with LEA support services. In some LEAs these proformas are made available on disc for use with the school's computer system. Hull (1995), Panter (1996) and Phillips and Cockett (1995) provide examples of proformas if you would like to compare those you use with those used elsewhere.

You have to decide which records *you* keep and store centrally and which will be managed by class teachers. The SEN Register is largely your responsibility, although, of course, teachers should be aware if any of their pupils are on the Register, and at which 'Stage' of provision they are recorded. Within each child's file, you may keep copies of their assessment and reports, and also their IEP. Teachers also need a copy of the IEP as this will inform their teaching. Monitoring progress will also be primarily their concern on a day-do-day basis, reporting to you if progress appears very slow (pupils appear not be meeting targets) or they need further advice. You need to devise a system which is easy to use *and* comprehensive. Consider also the position of any support assistant who may have a 'teaching role' and be in an excellent position to observe and report on a child's learning.

Some schools use coloured forms to distinguish stages of provision at a glance and ease the load. You must consider who has access to the records in deciding contents and storage arrangements.

Above all, records should be known to parents and reviewed regularly. Where children no longer require special help or move 'down' a stage, their records should be amended accordingly. This aspect is often overlooked, particularly where a child has presented behaviour difficulties and these have been dealt with successfully.

Managing the paperwork and records *is* time consuming and you may well be able to negotiate some time release to deal with this aspect. We know of some SENCOs who have half an hour each morning for controlling their paperwork and making necessary telephone calls while the rest of school is in assembly or the headteacher takes their class.

A good filing system is essential!

Organising and managing records

Central to organising and managing records are:

- There must be a clear relationship between the records to be kept and the procedures outlined in the school's policy.
- This relationship must be understood by all staff.
- Any system must make material easily accessible to staff (including professionals from external agencies) but be 'secure'.

There is no one way to do this. You could try developing **a computerised system**. This would include the SEN Register, copies of blank proformas and could include full IEPs for individual children. Primary schools are often at an earlier stage of developing computerised record-keeping and administrative systems because teachers may have limited access to IT and there are relatively small numbers of children with SEN compared with large secondary schools. However, bearing in mind that a primary SENCO usually also has a full teaching timetable, Stansfield's contention (1996) that the 'judicious use of Information Technology' can 'lighten the load' for SENCOs is worth exploring. Both Stansfield (1996) and NCET (1995) have reviewed IT packages for recording and monitoring progress in line with the Code of Practice. The recommendations of current practitioners can be sought through the SENCO forum web page.

Stansfield's criteria for selecting IT packages for administration of SEN procedures in a school:

- The package should include a hard disc with sufficient memory for the software to run easily, together with a good quality fast printer.
- The application should save time, not make more work than using traditional methods of recording. It should not take up valuable time which should be spent working with pupils.
- The package should be robust and not lose data or crash easily.
- It should be user-friendly for those SENCOs who may not be confident computer-users.
- It should have a password for data protection and sensitive information.
- It should be easily adaptable for the individual school needs.

It is worth mentioning here that information gathered on pupils on the SEN Register and the Code of Practice Stages, may be sensitive for pupils and parents. It is important that issues of confidentiality and sensitivity are borne in mind whatever recording system is being used and files should be kept securely.

Using a computerised system will probably mean that the SENCO will require access to support from the IT coordinator. You should also check with your adviser, or directly with the local data protection office, to ensure that in keeping the kind of information required for the SEN Register you are not contravening the Data Protection Act of 1984.

It is just as important that computer files are also securely held and should be protected by a password. Discs should also be held in a secure place, agreed between the SENCO and the headteacher, who is responsible for data protection. Stansfield also reminds us that the file containing the SEN Register should be removed from the hard disc except when it is being used.

Other types of filing systems include:
■ *A filing system* centrally stored, often using a colour coding system according to 'Stage' or provision, with open access for all staff.
■ *A filing system maintained only by the SENCO.*
■ *All individual files, including IEPs are maintained by class teachers.* The SENCO holds the SEN Register and records how each pupil's progress is to be monitored. The SENCO maintains a record of action taken to date, together with basic information, e.g. health, parents/carers, the involvement of other professionals, etc.

Maintaining the SEN Register

This should at least contain a list of the names of pupils, the dates on which the *concern* was registered and the 'Stage' at which they are placed. You may wish to keep further information (e.g. brief description of their SEN, date of IEP review).

Record of concern

N.B. the LEA may ask to see this Register as part of its local audit in allocating SEN funding and OFSTED Inspectors may also ask to see it. There should be a link between the SEN Register and the 'Record of Concern' at Stage 1.

At Stage 1 of the procedures there should be some record of concern which will form the basis for recording the child's name on the SEN Register and trigger your intervention. This might be very simple, as below. In some schools it is simply a one-line statement on the Class Register or SEN Register.

SEN Record of Concern

Name.. Year...

Concern

Action

Registered   Teacher...

Date..

Stage..

Review date: Date parents informed...

                                               Any comments from parents:

Any health difficulty known   SENCO — name and comment

Other Comments

Individual education plans (IEPs)

Chapter 9 is specifically concerned with writing IEPs.

Writing IEPs should be seen as the foundation of the intervention process in meeting SEN. What is important in managing procedures is to ensure that the IEP:

- sets clear learning objectives/targets for the pupil;
- states the current level of attainment;
- shows how these objectives are to be achieved, i.e. sets out strategies, resources, support;
- shows how the targets will be evaluated;
- provides evidence that the child and parents have not only been consulted, but their contribution to the programme is recorded where appropriate;
- establishes who will monitor the programme;
- states the review date.

This process, which involves several people at different times and may also involve a range of activities, requires planning ahead. The process for monitoring the child must be clear and easy to implement and a simple visual display (such as year planner or diary) is essential in tracking this process. An IEP can be viewed as the lynchpin of the process of assessment and intervention. The review of an IEP is itself a form of continuous assessment.

Reviews

By far the most challenging task for a SENCO is managing reviews, as there are implications for 'time' — the commodity most primary SENCOs do not have! The review process should be carried out regularly, and is often conducted by a class teacher and SENCO every half term, with parents being notified of progress rather than called to a review meeting. However, most schools try to include parents in reviews at least once a year, and some achieve this termly. It is perhaps worth listing here the recommendations of the Code of Practice for reviews at each stage.

Reviews: who is involved, what is involved:

You should refer to the Code for full details.

Stage 1 — Giving special help

Review dates — possibly within a term

     focus — progress made by the child
          — effectiveness of the special help
          — future action

    people — teacher (possibly with SENCO)
          — parents *informed* (should be spoken to in person if considering Stage 2 provision)

  outcome — the child continues at Stage 1
          — no longer requires special help
          — moves to Stage 2

Stage 2 — SENCO takes the lead

Review dates — within a term for first two reviews

     focus — progress made by the child
          — effectiveness of the IEP
          — contribution made by parents
          — updated information and advice
          — future action

    people — SENCO conducts review
          — teacher and any 'special' teacher/assistant
          — parents invited where possible, especially if moving to Stage 3

  outcome — parents must always be informed of outcome
          — continue at Stage 2
          — revert to Stage 1 or no longer needs special help
          — if possible is still unsatisfactory after two review periods, move to Stage 3

Stage 3 — School calls upon external support/advice

Review dates — within a term

     focus — progress made by child
          — effectiveness of the IEP
          — updated information and advice
          — future action
          — whether the child is likely, in future, to be referred for statutory assessment

    people — SENCO will lead
          — teacher/special assistant
          — external specialist
          — parents should be 'invited and encouraged' and must be told of outcome (where any question of referral for statutory assessment, parents should be consulted in person)

  outcome — continue at Stage 3
          — revert to Stage 1 or 2
          — the headteacher considers referring the child to the LEA for statutory assessment

Annual review meeting for children who have statements of SEN

The LEA is responsible for initiating the annual review which is a legal requirement. The LEA requires the headteacher to submit a report on the child, by a specified date, and must give at least two months' prior notice of that date. The regulations place much of this responsibility on the headteacher, who may delegate the responsibility for holding the review meeting to the SENCO under para. 6.8 of the Code of Practice. What follows, therefore, refers to the *headteacher*, but the duties may be carried out by the SENCO (or shared between head and SENCO, as appropriate).

Review date — set by LEA

focus — views of all professionals and parents as to child's progress
— updated information and advice
— reconsideration of appropriateness of statement
— amendments if necessary

people — headteacher/SENCO or relevant teacher must be invited Teacher/other involved professionals *may* be invited but *must* (or must be invited to) send appropriate reports
— child's parents (carers) must be invited
— LEA representative *must* be invited

outcome — amend statement
— cease to maintain

Preparing for a review meeting

This may be used as the basis for any case conference.

Advance preparation

1. Two months before meeting, the headteacher/SENCO must give notice of the meeting (date, time, venue, purpose) and request written advice from:
   ■ the child's parents;
   ■ anyone identified by the LEA;
   ■ others considered appropriate (e.g. personnel from health or social services who may be involved, as well as professionals from support services, e.g. visiting

specialist teachers, the educational psychologist), the class teacher, SENCO and Specialist Support Assistant involved.

It is important to give plenty of notice, not only so that those who may wish to attend can note the date, but so that the external professionals have time to observe and assess the child before writing a report. Check also that parents/carers are available on the dates you suggest (they may have to make arrangements for the care of other children or obtain leave of absence from work).

2. You may wish to invite the parents to meet with you and/or the class teacher, before the review, and this could be most helpful to them as they are likely to need support, particularly if this is the first review since a statement was provided. (Other 'key' times will be if the child is 'new' to your school or the review is to take place prior to a 'transition' to another school). An informal pre-review meeting helps the parents to prepare for the review, which may be stressful for them as it is:
    a) a formal occasion
    b) crucial to subsequent decisions about their child
    This is an opportunity to reassure them about the conduct of the review, help them to understand any terminology which may be used and discuss when and how they will make their contribution.

3. At least two weeks before the review meeting you should write to all those invited to attend, sending copies of all the written advice available and inviting additional written comments. Check that any of these reports are written in a way that parents can understand. Remind them of the date, time and venue of the meeting, asking them to confirm their intention to attend in order to help you prepare the occasion. Offer to meet them beforehand if they would like some help in understanding the reports.

    Ask child/parents whether or not the child wishes to attend for all or part of the meeting. Some primary schools invite the child only at a point where she/he could contribute a view on progress.

4. Make sure you have any copies of the child's work you would like to refer to during the meeting, together with extra copies of the papers circulated earlier in case some people forget to bring them.

You should also refer to Chapter 4 on Managing Meetings.

Holding the meeting

1. Make clear
   - the purpose of the annual review meeting;
   - that you will chair and write the report;
   - that the report will be circulated for comment and this will require a 'quick return' prior to being sent to the LEA;
   - that everyone will have an opportunity to speak and give their comments.
2. It is important to set the 'tone' of the meeting, in particular helping parents to feel comfortable with the situation.
3. You may then ask each of those present to refer to their report and provide comments.
4. You must make sure that the advice of any professional unable to attend is made known and considered.
5. The parents' views must be made known (either directly or through you or another teacher if they are unable to attend).
6. The child's views must be made known, either directly or through others (parents/carers, teachers, other professionals).

In chairing the meeting you have to ensure that the advice of all those concerned is heard and discussed. The members must:
- consider all evidence and advice;
- note any progress in learning that has been made;
- note any change in the child's situation (e.g. health, learning context, attainment);
- consider current provision;
- decide on appropriate targets for the coming year;
- consider the extent to which these can be met using existing provision, or whether the provision should be changed in some way, for example:
  — a reduction in support time
  — a change in grouping methods
  — introduction of different method of human or physical support;
- determine future action and who will be involved;
- decide whether to recommment that the statement:
  — is appropriate and should be continued
  — should be amended, and how
  — should cease to be maintained.

It is not in your power to make these decisions but you can make recommendations to the LEA. You must ensure that notes are kept, the outcome can be justified by what has happened, and that the final report makes this clear.

Contributing to Stage 4 assessment

At a Stage 3 Review, a decision may be taken to ask the LEA if they will undertake multidisciplinary assessment (Stage 4).

When this decision is reached, you should ensure that parents are fully informed and the procedure explained. Parents need to know:
■ the purpose of the assessment;
■ that the LEA may not agree to carry out the assessment;
■ that following such an assessment, the LEA could decide not to issue a statement;
■ their right to appeal to the SEN tribunal and the identity of the 'named person' in their LEA.

As financial cuts have been made, LEAs have increasingly laid down criteria both for Stage 4 assessments and for the issuing of statements. Some LEAs may require the completion of a proforma in requesting Stage 4 assessment. Unless a parent has already made the request, the Code of Practice states that it is a headteacher's responsibility to take the decision to make the request. Normally you, as SENCO, will be closely involved.

The LEA will require evidence of the pupil's SEN and what the school has so far done to meet those needs. The materials used as the basis of the Stage 3 review will be useful to you — copies of IEPs and review reports — together with a summary of the reasons for referral.

Schools are asked to contribute to the multi-disciplinary assessment by completing 'Appendix D' of the assessment. This appendix, which is part of the advice and assessment used by the LEA in reaching a decision as to whether or not to issue a statement, will become part of the 'Statement' if one is issued.

Most LEAs provide a proforma for completion, and it is customary for a SENCO or headteacher to complete it. Advice from a visiting support teacher could also be attached.

> **Advice for Stage 4 assessment:**
>
> Provide the following information:
>
> *Background information*: Child's age; how long the child has been in your school; summarise, with dates, the child's progress through Stages 1–3 and list any special provision made (if you have developed a simple 'SEN Record' as described earlier in this Chapter, this information will be available).
>
> *Other information* which may be useful: e.g. medical information, attendance record, parental support.
>
> *Current attainments*: List the child's strengths and weaknesses in different areas. Make reference to National Curriculum attainments, indicating levels, and showing whether/not these are teacher assessments. It is important to include literacy (reading, writing, spelling), numeracy, language and communication skills, social skills and behaviour, together with how the child relates to adults and peers.
>
> In addition it is useful to note the child's preferred learning styles and attitude to school/separate subject areas where significant.
>
> *Special Educational Needs*: using the above information, summarise your view of the child's strengths and SEN. *Be specific*.
>
> *Aims of provision*: state what you consider would be the aim of special provision, based on the above.
>
> *Resources*: Suggest the resources/special provision which you believe necessary for the child to fulfil these aims. Refer to teaching support and equipment, e.g. IT, as appropriate.

Records of SEN procedures

You need to try to reduce paperwork for yourself and colleagues to a minimum, whilst at the same time ensuring that your proformas contain all necessary information to facilitate meeting SEN with regard to the Code of Practice. You will find it useful, therefore, to keep a Record of SEN Progress on each child which is related to the SEN Record of Concern, but is perhaps stored at the front of each child's file. Keeping to our 'rule' which is always to try to use only a sheet of A4 paper where possible, we suggest this contains:

- basic information about the child (name, date of birth, parent/carer contact, schools attended and dates);
- date when concern was registered;
- summary of reason for concern;
- SEN stages with dates/review dates;
- any external agencies involved.

Your record might look like this:

SEN Progress Record   **Side 1**

Child's name...Date of Birth...

Parents/Carers: names..

Contact address...

....

Home language...

Date of Initial Registration of Concern...

Reason for Concern...

....

Schools attended...

....

LEA...Dates..

Health/any other information..

....

SEN STAGES   **Side 2**
Stage   **Comments**   **Review Dates**

Services	Comments	Dates
External/Support Service Involvement		
Services	**Comments**	**Dates**

This sort of form will reduce the amount of information you need to transfer to each IEP. It will also be a useful source of evidence if you do need to request assessment at Stage 4. It will also be invaluable should you be required to prepare evidence for a tribunal.

Preparation for SEN tribunals

The SEN Tribunal was set up by the 1993 Education Act to consider parents' appeals against decisions of the LEA about their children's SEN. An appeal should, of course, only come about where there has been failure to agree, and many appeals could perhaps be avoided by ensuring good communication between LEA and parents.

Parents' rights to appeal are stated in a DFE publication *SEN Tribunals: How to appeal* (DFE 1994b), which also indicates the areas which may not form the basis of an appeal.

Parents' rights:

Parents have the right to appeal if the LEA:
- refuse to carry out a formal assessment of a child's special educational needs but only if parents rather than the school have asked the LEA to carry out an assessment
- refuse to issue a statement of a child's SEN after making a formal assessment

If the LEA have made a statement of a child's special educational needs or have changed a previous statement, parents can appeal against:
- the description in Part II of the statement of a child's SEN
- the description in Part III of the special educational help that the LEA think the child should get
- the school named in Part IV of the statement
- or the LEA's decision not to name a school in Part IV

They can also appeal if the following apply:
- LEA refuse to change the school named in the statement (but only if the statement is a year old)
- the LEA refuse to reassess a child if there has not been a new assessment for at least six months (but only if the parent asked for the reassessment)
- the LEA decide not to maintain the statement any longer
- after reassessing the child, the LEA do not amend the statement

SEN Tribunals do have considerable power. A tribunal is chaired by a lawyer, and has two lay members who will have some professional experience of SEN. It can require witnesses to attend and can ask for access to a child's records to provide evidence of special educational need. Sometimes a headteacher or the SENCO (or both) may attend, and this may be at the request of the LEA *or* parents. It is not unknown for a SENCO to be asked to be a witness at a tribunal on behalf of both parties, as often it is a SENCO who has the greatest knowledge of the child's needs and the ability of the school to make appropriate provision.

At times, schools might believe that the parents are justified in appealing against the LEA. This occurs particularly where staff consider they need more support than they can provide from within their own resources. At other times, however, they might agree with the LEA and believe that the child's needs are being met appropriately. Many SENCOs and headteachers view an appeal to a tribunal as a conflict situation: emotions heighten and they feel under considerable stress. (Indeed some heads and teachers have asked to be 'subpoenaed' to attend, in order to reduce the likelihood of being seen to 'take sides'.)

However, you should not feel there is conflict or be unduly stressed. A tribunal exists to try to protect a child's entitlement to appropriate educational provision. Your professional advice is necessary to any discussion on this matter and you should try to avoid a confrontational stance. Tribunals are formal occasions, but every attempt is made to conduct them without an adversarial atmosphere. You should, therefore, maintain your professional relationships with all concerned — after all, you are going to have to work cooperatively with both the parents and the LEA after the tribunal!

You will need to prepare yourself for the hearing. You may be asked to provide records and reports in advance — the IEP is always a very important document. If your SEN practices are sound, this should not involve you in any extra work as you will have up-do-date information on the child's progress. If you attend the tribunal in person, you need to be prepared to answer questions on:

> Tribunals are very stressful events for parents, who feel particularly disappointed if their appeals are not upheld.

- how the school's SEN policy operates
- how the school allocates resources from the SEN budget*
- how IEPs are monitored
- how work is differentiated
- how support is organised in general, and for this particular pupil (including time allocated, nature of the work and personnel involved).

(* Do you *know* this? Finding out about how the SEN budget is allocated and your role in managing is a major responsibility for a SENCO — see below. This contentious issue is worth investigating with your headteacher and governors.)

Clearly every attempt should be made to prevent the disagreements and misunderstandings which lead to parental appeals. As a SENCO you have a role in helping parents/carers to understand *at every stage*, what is being done for the child and how this relates to their child's needs. 'Partnership with parents' also means helping them to feel empowered and aware of what resources and sources of support are available to them. The ability to refer them to local and national voluntary organisations, parent support groups and appropriate LEA personnel is central to *your* role in supporting parents. It is useful, therefore, to keep a list of appropriate agencies who can provide useful information, not only for you and colleagues, but also for parents — see Chapter 14. You can also advise them how to obtain the booklet on advice about appeals and the SEN Tribunal (from the LEA or DFE).

Finding out about the school's SEN budget and how it is used

The headteacher and governor designated for SEN should be able to clarify this for you — and indeed in some schools it is made explicit in their SEN policy document. You should not confuse the SEN 'budget' with the amount of money you are allocated to spend annually on teaching materials (capitation allowance). SEN allowances are awarded by the LEA in relation to certain criteria Often the money is allocated in relation to free school meals, literacy or SATs levels and number of pupils identified by the LEA as having need for extra provision over and above that which the school can provide. In addition there may be further resources such as full- or part-time learning support assistants who are part of the SEN 'provision' identified on a pupil's statement, special equipment (e.g. a computer) or advisory support from external agencies.

Some of the income may be earmarked for salaries, or parts of salaries, by your school (for example, part of your salary may come from this, or the school may employ part-time teachers or learning support assistants). You need to be aware of what the total income is and how it is used to meet the needs of those for whom it is intended.

You should obtain/or at least have sight of a written statement about the budget. OFSTED and any audit by the Audit Commission would also need access to this.

Part two Managing teaching and learning

Chapter 6   Managing identification and assessment

The assessment procedures used for identifying and meeting SEN must be integrated within your school's assessment policy. Most teachers now accept that assessment is part of the normal teaching process and it should be clear from earlier chapters that the identification and assessment of SEN is part of the intervention process (and an integrated part of writing and reviewing IEPs).

A major concern for teachers centres on *decision making*: when (and on what evidence) should a class teacher 'register a concern'? At what point should they seek advice from a SENCO? What serves as a 'trigger'? There are decisions where the SENCO's views may be particularly important, e.g. deciding, after reviews, whether to maintain a child at the same stage or move to the next stage. Similarly a major decision must be made whether, at an early stage of identification, to recommend that the child must be registered at Stage 3 or 4 without proceeding through the stages, because of severity of the difficulty.

Clearly experience and training will help you to make decisions. Significant discrepancies between a child's performance and that of peers is one form of trigger, and assessing attainment within the National Curriculum provides much important information. You will also need to build an assessment resource for SEN using informal and published materials.

Before writing the SEN assessment policy and selecting your assessments, you should ask yourself several questions.
- Why are we assessing? (Purpose)
- What are we trying to assess?
- How will we assess this?
- Who will undertake the assessment?
- Which children will be assessed?
- When will they be assessed?
- How will the information be used?

These simple questions are often neglected. They are useful in reviewing your school assessment policy as a whole, but the discussion here focuses on relevance to SEN and we suggest that you give them some thought.

Why are we assessing?

Assessment is significant for discovering what children can do, their attainments and learning strengths as well as difficulties. Primary School Standard Attainment Tests (SATs) at the end of Key Stages 1 and 2 provide broad guidance for comparing standards and identifying pupils with very low attainments. Teachers' assessments of children's levels within each Key Stage (KS) of the National Curriculum are important sources of information about a child's learning, indicating their needs in terms of access to the curriculum.

Curriculum-based assessment is used by all teachers and you need to encourage them to realise its value in relation to identifying SEN, writing and monitoring IEPs, and planning the curriculum. In addition you may use other forms of assessment procedures, teacher-made and published materials, both criterion and norm-referenced tests in order to determine the nature of the difficulties and throw light on how the child learns most successfully.

Gipps (1994) suggests that there are two main ways of classifying the purposes of assessment — managerial and professional. By 'managerial' she means the use of assessment to help manage/organise education systems, whereas 'professional' implies using assessment to improve teaching and learning.

Managerial uses therefore would include:

- *baseline* testing on school (or stage) entry;
- *selection* processes (allocating pupils to particular schools or learning groups/classes);
- *National Curriculum Assessment* (SATs) to monitor standards in schools.

Professional uses include:

- *screening* (to identify pupils' needs);
- *diagnostic testing* (to identify the strengths and weaknesses of individual children);
- *testing for monitoring/evaluating progress*;
- *records of achievement* (to provide evidence of progress and provide feedback to individuals of achievements over a range of areas).

These distinctions are not always clear in the field of SEN, for often managerial decisions such as referral for multidisciplinary assessment at Stage 4 or the Code of Practice, or requests for disapplication of aspects of the National Curriculum, may be based on your 'professional' assessments. Similarly baseline assessment on school entry will also serve a 'screening' function. However, you may find this classification useful in clarifying your *purposes* in assessing. It is important not to 'test' if you can obtain the assessment information you require whilst you are teaching. This not only prevents duplication of effort (and saves time), but also means the child does not begin to feel 'tested' rather than 'taught and helped'.

In considering the purposes of testing you might find an earlier typology useful (Macintosh and Hale, 1976).

Suggestion

Clarifying your thinking on the purpose of assessment

List what seem to you to be the main purposes in assessment in the area of SEN and identify how your school addresses each of them.

Are the purposes of assessment the same for all children? Might some children be the subject of more assessment than others? How is this justified?

Six major purposes of assessment:

Diagnosis — to determine nature of learning difficulties
Evaluating — reviewing learning/teaching strategies
Grading — to compare standards (including ipsatively)
Guidance — to help pupils make a decision about work, career, options
Selection — to allocate to particular groups
Prediction — to forecast an outcome

What are we trying to assess?

The *emphasis* must be on strengths and weaknesses in:
- all curriculum areas;
- the child's learning styles;

and *particularly* their strengths and difficulties in:
- literacy and numeracy skills (as these often affect access and progress within the curriculum as well as being the two major areas of the primary curriculum);

and *possibly* strengths and weaknesses in:
- areas considered to underpin learning such as phonological awareness, visual memory and sequencing skills.

It is important to distinguish between the direct assessment of performance in classroom-based activities (such as reading and spelling) and assessment of 'assumed underlying abilities' (such as IQ and perceptuo-motor abilities), where such assumptions are, in any case, controversial. The former assessments are of greater use to teachers, although there may be occasions when you wish to take account of the latter.

Assessment should always take into account not only a child's perceived 'needs', but his/her educational needs in relation to the demands of the curriculum. Consider a child's ability to function within a particular context as this will then help you to address how to support the child and how to make the curriculum more accessible.

How will we assess this?

As a SENCO you will probably have major responsibility for deciding which assessment methods to use for:
— screening/identifying
— assessing difficulties (diagnostic testing)

and for establishing a record-keeping system related to the SEN Register and IEPs. Choosing methods and tests will, of course, be in consultation with colleagues, and in particular the subject coordinators for literacy and maths. You will also

It is as important when carrying out the assessment of any individual child to ask the first question in the Activity on p. 103 as it is when drawing up your SEN assessment procedures.

The answer to the first two questions in the Activity on p. 103 for any child should help you to select only the most appropriate techniques and prevent you from over-assessing a child.

A major aspect of the assessment process must be to involve the child before undertaking testing. Very often talking to the child may throw light on the problem — perhaps even removing the need for further assessment. It may, however, suggest areas for assessment which had not previously been considered.

have to agree as to which procedures/materials you will use and which will be used by classroom teachers.

Main approaches to assessment

The literature on assessment distinguishes three main categories:

- norm-referenced tests
- criterion-referenced tests
- ipsative testing (describing a process rather than tests)

You need to be aware of these differences when you are addressing all the questions listed at the beginning of this chapter, not only 'How will I assess this?'

Classifying assessment

Norm-referenced tests
— express a result in relation to peers, e.g. reading age or IQ result (useful for comparison with others)

Criterion-references tests
— express as a result about what has or has not been learned in relation to a specified task (useful in planning what to teach next)

Ipsative testing
— gathers information about performance in relation to that individual's other performance in the same domain (shows progress) or across other domains (to give a learning profile)

Black (1997) provides a critical discussion of these approaches. As a SENCO you are likely to use all three. In particular you are concerned that a pupil makes improvement and therefore *ipsative* assessment is central to your work and SEN philosophy.

Norm-referenced tests are often used for screening purposes, particularly at Key Stage 2, where discrepancies between a child's scores and those of peers signal a need for further exploration. Norm-reference tests often tell you little about the nature of a child's difficulty and, therefore, are not very useful diagnostically, although there are some notable exceptions, particularly the Neale Analysis of Reading Ability and the New Macmillan Reading Test where the use of miscue analysis is incorporated.

The majority of diagnostic tests are criterion-referenced. These will help to identify specific aspects of difficulty and also indicate tasks where a child has strengths. Where there is a logical sequence, and rationale underpinning the criteria used, then such tests can be very useful in helping you to set learning targets for the pupil. Teachers can devise their own criterion-referenced tests in relation to their teaching. The new National Literacy Strategy, for example, provides a detailed framework which lends itself easily to establishing tasks (as part of the normal teaching–learning process) which can be used to identify strengths and weaknesses. Some criterion-referenced tests may take the form of a checklist or rating scale to identify strengths and weaknesses in certain areas. Two particularly useful screening instruments are the Bury Infant Checklist (Pearson and Quinn, 1986) and the Infant Rating Scale (Lindsay, 1981). Devising checklists can become very time-consuming both in development and in completing and interpreting. We all know of some schools which have generated lengthy checklists where concise reports from a teacher based on their observations would be more useful to a SENCO.

Tests also vary as to whether they are administered to groups or individuals.

Group Tests
- a whole class/year group can be assessed at the same time;
- many have a set time limit;
- usually easy to administer and score;
- often, but not always, norm-referenced;
- may take various forms (e.g. multiple choice, answer-completion);
- often known as 'pencil and paper' tests, usually requiring a written response (or underlining or a mark put on paper) and often, *but not always*, requiring reading skills.

Individual Tests
- one child only at a time;
- occasionally timed: the majority are untimed;

- may be norm-referenced;
- it is possible to observe the child during the assessment process;
- often of greater diagnostic value than a group test;
- may take various forms.

How to choose tests

Published tests and assessment materials can be very useful but you must choose wisely within your overall policy. Publishers' catalogues will help you to discover what is available. (That of NFER-Nelson is particularly informative.) It is very important as a SENCO that you become familiar with the *manual* for any test in order to ascertain:

- *what* it purports to assess;
- the age range for which the test was devised;
- the date of publication (if it has been updated, in what way has it changed? The language of tests can quickly become dated or show cultural/gender bias.);
- if it is a norm-referenced test, whether the population on which the test was standardised was similar to the one you are assessing, and whether it is a valid and reliable test (see Black, 1997);
- what instructions there are for
  — administration
  — scoring
- how useful the information obtained will be for planning teaching.

Checklists for identification of special educational needs

A further aspect of your assessment resources will be checklists which help you and other teachers to identify a range of special educational needs. In many cases such checklists are provided for schools by specialist support services. The two provided here are for guidance in identifying hearing or visual difficulties, but your local support services or educational psychologist may supply a range of such materials (for example, for identifying specific learning difficulties such as dyslexia or dyspraxia, communication and speech difficulties, behaviour difficulties and autistic spectrum disorders).

Checklist — identification of possible visual difficulties:

- holds reading material at unusual distance or angle
- screws up eyes/face when reading from blackboard (or books)
- difficulties in copying from board (or book)
- peers at objects
- may appear clumsy: walks into objects
- rubs eyes frequently
- may lose place when reading
- often omits letters or words when reading or copying
- confuses visually similar words or letters (e.g. h and b)
- tires easily when work involves reading or copying
- very slow in tasks requiring reading or copying
- may misbehave or not settle down to work which requires visual skills

Checklist — identification of possible hearing difficulties:

- may not reply when spoken to, or gives inappropriate response
- often asks for question/instruction to be repeated or says 'pardon'
- may appear to ignore or forget what a teacher asks
- performance deteriorates over the day (from 'effort' of listening)
- may appear to be day-dreaming or have 'switched off'
- may watch a speaker's face intently
- frequent colds/absence for cold: often has catarrh
- suffers from ear infections
- spelling may reflect omitted letters, letter confusion
- may speak very loudly and/or in monotone
- difficulty in acquiring phonic skills in reading and spelling
- may misbehave, get frustrated and irritable
- may appear 'in a world of own'

All assessment procedures form part of the SEN resources you have to manage (see Chapter 7), but it is important that the role of SENCO does not emphasise assessment at the expense of meeting children's special educational needs. Assessment is simply a means to that end. As you will need expertise and experience in both selecting and using assessment procedures over and beyond those used by your colleagues, you have to resist being placed in a position where other staff see you as the person responsible for *all* SEN assessment. Similarly it is important to make assessment 'user-friendly' for your colleagues by demystifying procedures. In the same way, you should ensure that any assessment undertaken by a pupil causes as little anxiety as possible for that child (and parents). Many procedures offer advice as to how this can be done. Many SENCOs would advise that you discuss any assessment fully with the child in advance — explaining how it is designed for *you* to find out the 'best way' for teaching so she/he can learn — and that you follow this up by showing how it has done this, by setting a target jointly with the pupil.

It is very important that, in managing resources, you pay particular attention to Test Manuals as these are essential to remind you of the test's purposes, advantages and limitations, and the need to follow the precise test procedures as stated.

The power of observation

Most SENCOs agree that developing observation skills and training others (teachers and support assistants) to observe provides the school's most significant assessment resource. Observation skills involve an ability to record what can actually be seen without adding your own interpretation. An example of interpretation rather than observation can be seen in the comments 'Sally is day-dreaming' or 'Ben is not listening'. Both show evidence of interpretation which often *reflects* a cultural bias and personal values. Similarly it is important to build up a picture from several observations and there are many different approaches to using observation as part of the assessment process. You will find the book *A Practical Guide to Child Observation* (Hobart and Frankel, 1997) particularly useful if you have not had any training in observation. Although it draws on examples from working with very young children, the principles and techniques may be used across age ranges.

Curriculum-based assessment

Curriculum areas are best assessed as part of the class teacher's normal teaching–observing–assessing–teaching cycle using informal methods and, of course, SATs where appropriate. This should include consideration of a child's attainments with and without 'support', e.g. some children may demonstrate a higher level of understanding when

FIG 6.1
A model of the
teaching–assessment–teaching cycle

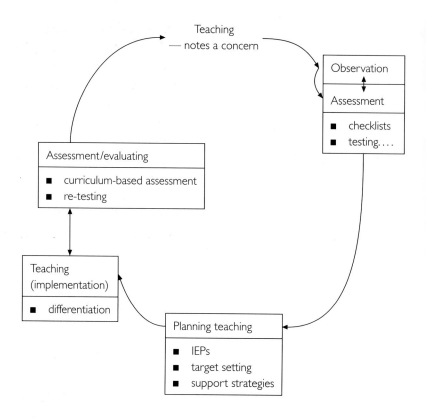

a question is read to them than they would if they had to read it themselves.

Teaching and assessment should not be seen as two separate activities, as the process of teaching involves continuous assessment of our pupils — we respond to how they behave during our teaching. We continually observe, interpret and make judgments about how they are learning, based on interpreting non-verbal behaviour, the oral answers they give (or lack of reply) to our questions, and our marking and evaluation of their products. We make adjustments both during the act of teaching and in later planning. The model (Figure 6.1) is familiar to many teachers and is the basis also for the assessment of SEN under the Code of Practice. A teacher becomes concerned about a pupil and may be able, through flexible teaching and 'differentiation', to meet the child's needs so that there is no further difficulty or concern. It may be, however, that the teacher makes further observation and may, with your assistance, carry out more formal assessment leading to the identification of learning needs and targets to be met.

These may be met satisfactorily by the class teacher using differentiation strategies. The teacher continues to monitor progress during teaching (evaluating/assessing). The model is still appropriate at later stages of the Code of Practice, although you are likely to be more involved during both the assessment and planning stage (and even, perhaps, involved in some of the implementation and teaching). You will also be involved in monitoring and reviewing progress. However, discussion of the use of a cyclical model of assessment and teaching with other staff helps them appreciate that many of their responsibilities under the Code of Practice can be managed with only minor alterations to their everyday practices.

Clearly you have to relate this to the school's SEN procedures as to how and where you will become involved in supporting the teaching/assessment cycle.

Teachers' judgments

A major issue in identifying SEN is whether a teacher's judgment is reliable, or whether more 'objective' measures should be used. Teachers themselves may feel insecure about this: how often have you heard teachers say that they don't read a report on a child passed by a previous teacher, in case it is misleading, 'labels' a child and adversely affects how *they* view the child? We must try to change this perspective by becoming more professional in making the assessments, and writing about them. It may often be useful, therefore, to draw on a variety of sources of information to 'check out' our perceptions of concern.

A further issue arises from the fact that teachers often notice certain behaviours such as low attention span, restlessness and turning round in seats and begin to associate these with learning difficulties. This leads to the possibility that if these behaviours are used as 'indicators' then the special educational needs of children who do not exhibit such behaviours may be overlooked.

Thus in addressing the question as to 'how' to assess, you will need to consider using a range of formal and informal methods, teachers' assessments and published materials

including norm- and criterion-referenced tests and checklists.
Your selection of procedures should be guided by the
following principles: that they

- meet the purposes of SEN assessment in the areas required;
- are easy to administer, record, (score where appropriate) and interpret;
- yield useful and reliable information;
- help you (and other teachers) to set targets for a child and plan appropriate teaching.

Who will undertake the assessment?

This question has been partly addressed above and in
Chapter 5. It is likely that class teachers will carry out most
of the assessment, particularly in relation to performance in
the curriculum. In schools where you use a screening process,
particularly based on 'group' testing, then the class teacher
will be involved. You should consider how the classroom
assistants and learning support assistants can become involved
in observation of children, in completing checklists and in
carrying out short activities (under your direction) to identify
particular strengths and difficulties. As SENCO you will
perhaps be directly involved in diagnostic, individual
assessment, although often class teachers prefer to do this
themselves if it is 'manageable' as they have closer knowledge
of the child.

Where you do undertake any assessment for a teacher,
it is, of course, essential to pass on detailed information
and recommendations for teaching and any other action you
believe appropriate, such as suggesting the involvement of a
support assistant in teaching, or the use of particular materials
or teaching methods.

It may well be that when you report back your assessments
to the teacher there are some differences between her concerns
and assessments and yours. Such discrepancies are not
unusual and may result from a range of factors:

- Different forms of assessment: different skills and abilities are being assessed, for example, different aspects of reading (decoding isolated words compared with reading in context).

- The assessments were carried out
  - in different situations (busy classroom compared with a quiet room and a one-to-one situation);
  - at a different time of day (child put more/less effort in; tiredness or even hunger could be factors).
- Child paid more attention or took greater care in one situation.
- Assessment materials were more/less motivating.
- The relationships between the child and the assessors were different.

You may find similar differences when an assessment is carried out by an external agency such as the Educational Psychologist or a Learning Support Teacher. It is important to draw on your interpersonal skills and knowledge of assessment and the child in order to explain different results. Where you can find no explanation you may need to undertake further observations and assessments.

Which children will be assessed?

Clearly there will be times when *all* children in a class or year group will be assessed — on entry to a school and at the ages of 7 and 11 in relation to the National Curriculum. However, whatever processes you use for screening and identification you have to make a decision about which children should be further assessed to determine their needs.

All children on the SEN Register should have been assessed — but methodologies will vary according to how you answer the first two questions.

When will they be assessed?

In addition to the occasions when *all* children are assessed there will be certain times when children on the SEN Register will be assessed. A key point will be when a pupil is not making progress at Stage 1 of the Code of Practice and assessment is needed to prepare an IEP (or determine whether there is a need to 'fast-track' to Stages 3 or 4). Any later assessment will normally be based on analysing progress for review or referring to external agencies for advice or assessment of another professional, e.g. an Educational Psychologist.

How will the information be used?

A good assessment will lead directly to recommendations for teaching, including setting targets. The summary of your assessment should be discussed with the class teacher (and anyone else involved in teaching or supporting the child) and the parents/carers and child, where appropriate.

You might also be asked to prepare an assessment report for another professional (for example by a Learning Support Service) and at Stage 4 you will, of course, be required to contribute towards statutory assessment.

Information to put in an assessment report:

Child's name, Date of Birth, Chronological Age.

Reason for referral: major cause for concern.

Any known medical condition.

Information about
- forms of assessment carried out including dates (and scores where applicable)
- National Curriculum levels (indicating SATS and teacher assessments)
- the results of any diagnostic assessments showing strengths and weaknesses

Recommendations for teaching including learning objectives/targets

You should sign and date your report.

Assessment in the early years (nursery and KS1)

Some children's special educational needs may have been identified at a very early age and records passed on at entry to nursery or infant school. This is particularly true where a child has severe learning difficulties, or a physical disability, health disorder or sensory impairment. Even if your school has no provision for children under the age of 5; you should familiarise yourself with the relevant sections of the Code of Practice. It is likely that such children will have been receiving a range of multi-professional support, perhaps involving a number of agencies and individuals who do not normally work with your school. Some young children may have been attending a Child Development Centre or have been assessed by several services (health, education and social services), which are part of a Local Authority's provision for early years. Usually there will be substantial records available.

When *all* children enter school, it is important to draw on information from parents/carers. Your school will have a policy on this, and it may be that such information is sought at an interview or there may be a request for a written account. Hinton (1993) describes Wolfendale's development of a Learning Profile (All About Me) designed for use at school entry, which is completed by a parent in conjunction with their child. This record covers seven areas of development:

- language
- playing and learning
- self-help
- physical development
- health and habits
- behaviour and social development
- moods and feelings

Your school may well have produced something similar — we know of schools where parents and children complete pictures and charts to indicate achievements. As SENCO you should make use of the school's entry records in order to identify children 'at risk' and follow up concerns with parents as soon as possible.

Records for young children should include profiles across a range of areas of development and early learning (particularly literacy and numeracy skills) and be based on observations made and information gathered on several occasions because their performance fluctuates so greatly.

Using baseline assessment as part of the SEN procedures

All primary schools will introduce baseline assessment from September 1998, and, whilst this may raise some concerns about misuse, many teachers welcome the fact that it can help a school to monitor its own effectiveness. Many primary schools have used some form of early assessment for a number of years, and it serves a valuable function for a SENCO in that it identifies, at an early stage, those children who may experience difficulties. It is important, of course, to remember that children at this age are at varying developmental stages, with differing rates of development. Similarly, just as baseline assessment reflects what a child knows and understands on school entry (a major purpose of the assessment) it is important to recognise that this will have been affected by the child's background and learning experiences to date. You, therefore, have information on which you can base:

■ some concern (there may be a special need);
■ your teaching strategies;
■ discussion with parents;
■ discussion with a class teacher;
■ a monitoring process.

In other words, do not assume that children have difficulties in learning until you are sure they have had access to appropriate teaching. You may then need to follow this with further diagnostic testing and observation, so that if you decide a child should be put on the SEN Register, you can build up a learning profile/record using a range of sources.

Baseline assessment/profiling at reception should include information about:

■ Social and emotional competence
■ Communication skills
■ Self-help/independence skills
■ Motor skills
■ Literacy and numeracy skills
■ Conceptual/reasoning skills

appropriate to the age group. Materials should be evaluated in terms of racial and gender bias, as noted earlier, and you must

As stated earlier, the SEN assessment procedures must be fully integrated with (and make use of where possible) the whole school procedures to avoid duplication of work in assessment and recording.

take these factors into account when you interpret results. Similarly, some children who perform well on entry, may do so because they have had formal preschool education (e.g. in a nursery) or have had very favourable home circumstances or developed at a different rate from others. Some of these children may continue to learn effectively, but some may experience difficulties later. Your assessment and monitoring procedures must be capable of identifying these children. Useful though baseline assessment is, it will not be able to predict difficulties which emerge subsequently.

If there are concerns at an early stage, then the child's name should be put on the SEN Register. This will ensure that their development is monitored and if they make satisfactory progress then their names can be removed after six months. 'Triggers' for adding a name to the Register at this stage would be:

- significant language delay
- speech/articulation difficulties affecting intelligibility
- delay in achieving 'normal development' in physical skills communication, social and cognitive functioning, including 'play'.

Assessment at Key Stage 2

In this phase you will be able to draw on information from Year 2 SATs and other KS1 information. You will need to liaise closely with the feeder primary school if your school is a junior school, not an all-age primary. You might draw on some of the principles concerning liaison at transition to secondary school which are made later in this chapter in relation to preparing for the new intake well in advance, and meeting and reassuring parents.

At KS2 you can draw on a wide range of published materials in addition to teachers' assessments. Published tests for children 7–11 normally provide more reliable information than those for a younger age range. The following list is not intended to be comprehensive but reflects those most commonly used by primary SENCOs known to us.

A useful source book is *Assessing Individual Needs* (Ayers, et al., 1996).

Useful resources for SEN assessment in Primary Schools

Title	Publisher	Suitable for ages
General ability/development		
All about Me	Nottingham Ed. Supplies	3–6
Aston Portfolio (including handwriting)	LDA, Wisbech	5–12
British Picture Vocabulary Scale (2nd edition)	NFER–Nelson	2–13
Bury Infant Checklist	NFER–Nelson	5–6
Concepts of Print Test (Clay)	NFER–Nelson	3–7
(COPS, for use on PC)		5–8
Early Years Easy Screen	NFER–Nelson	2–6
Infant Rating Scale	Hodder & Stoughton	5–7
Portage Early Education Programme	NFER–Nelson	0–6
Reading		
Macmillan Group Reading (Screening)	NFER–Nelson	5–9
Individual Reading Analysis	NFER–Nelson	5–10
Neale Analysis of Reading Ability	NFER–Nelson	5–13
Teach Yourself to Diagnose Reading Difficulties	NFER–Nelson	5–13
Get Reading Right (Phonic Skills)	Gibson	5–13
Maths/Numeracy		
Early Diagnosis of Maths Difficulties	NFER–Nelson	5–8
Yardsticks	NFER–Nelson	5–10
Spelling		
Graded Word Spelling Test (Vernon)	Hodder & Stoughton	5–11
Spelling in Context (Peters and Smith)	NFER–Nelson	5–13

Transition to secondary school

Most secondary schools have established good relations and transition procedures with their main feeder primary schools. It is important that there is good liaison between you and the

SENCO of the secondary school so that there can be continuity of support for pupils with SEN. The Code of Practice is clear that 'schools should make full use of information passed to them when the pupil transfers between phases' (DFE, 1994, para 2.17).

You should liaise with the secondary school SENCO (and there may well be several secondary schools involved) to discuss the nature of the information which will be most useful for the secondary school. This should include IEPs, assessment data and information about preferred learning styles, emotional and social development, the nature of learning support provided in the primary school and the nature of relationships between the school and parents. Many secondary SENCOs try to visit, observe and meet Year 6 pupils with SEN prior to transfer and some make arrangements to meet parents. As a primary SENCO you can play a major role in reassuring both the children with SEN and their parents/carers about the process of transfer to the secondary sector. You can also facilitate the secondary SENCO's role by inviting him/her to plan the transition process jointly with you. It would, for example, be appropriate to invite the secondary SENCO to any Year 6 annual review meetings. Similarly, *you* need to know what the arrangements are for meeting SEN in the secondary schools so that you can answer parents' questions with confidence. If a parent sees that you know about a secondary school's provision, they are more likely to have confidence in that school than if your response is, 'You must ask the secondary SENCO'.

Questions for you to ask the Secondary SENCO(s)

1. How is SEN provision organised in the school? What support is available?
2. What role do you play in teaching and assessment of Year 7 pupils?
3. How is information about children with SEN made known to subject teachers?
4. Who will have direct responsibility for supporting a pupil with SEN? To whom do pupils go to if they are upset/anxious?
5. What are the arrangements for involving parents?
6. What links are there with external support agencies?

Finally, you might like to review practices as suggested below:

Reviewing your school's practices for SEN assessments:

Ask yourself the following questions:
1. What are the purposes of assessment of SEN?
2. What forms of assessment are currently used?
3. What use is made of
   — baseline assessment?
   — SATS information
   — teachers' assessments in maths and English?
4. What other forms of assessment are used
   — by class teachers?
   — by you as SENCO?
5. How useful are they? (Do they provide information which leads to strategies for teaching?)
6. Do you use information passed to you from other teachers and parents?
7. What arrangements exist for you to pass on information from any assessments *you* carry out
   — to class teachers
   — to parents
   — to the secondary school at transition or any school a pupil may transfer to
8. How do you use the information to write an IEP and set targets?
9. How do you monitor and record progress?
10. Are you satisfied, from your answers to the above, that your assessment procedures are effective? If not, what *changes* are necessary?

General references on assessment

AYERS, H., CLARKE, D. et al. (1996) *Assessing Individual Needs: A Practical Approach (2nd ed)*, London: David Fulton.

BLACK, P. (1997) *Testing: Friend or Foe? Theory and Practice of Assessment and Testing*, London: Falmer Press.

DUNCAN, A. and DUNN, W. (1988) *What Primary Teachers Should Know About Assessment*, London: Hodder and Stoughton.
(Good simple overview, with particularly good examples on maths assessment.)

GIPPS, C. and STOBART, G. (1993) *Assessment: A Teacher's Guide to the Issues*, London: Hodder and Stoughton.

HOBART, C. and FRANKEL, J. (1994) *A Practical Guide to Child Observation*, London: Stanley Thornes.
(Very practical guide. Emphasis on early years but the principles and techniques can be applied to *all* ages.)

Chapter 7   Managing resources

All too often the complaint of teachers and parents is that
SEN provision is 'resource driven' rather than 'needs based'.
It is a fact that finite resources are available and that schools,
LEA and support services must cooperate in order to maximise
the 'efficient' use of resources. A major element of efficiency
is, of course, effectiveness. An important fact of the SEN
coordinator's responsibility is the allocation and management
of resources — human, physical, time and financial. It is vital
to have an agreed strategy relating the allocation of resources
to the school's policy.

You need to know how much money is allocated to your
school for making SEN provision, and, in particular, to know
exactly what resources have been specifically allocated to any
pupil with a statement of SEN (this entitlement should be
specified on the statement). LEAs vary in their allocation of
funding to schools, but it is important to note that:

- in the budget allocated to your school there will be an
  identified amount for SEN;
- there will be funding according to special needs AWPU
  (age-weighted pupil unit) based on a local authority audit
  (often related to the number of pupils who have free school
  meals *or* according to number of children who require
  considerable support for their SEN. Many LEAs have
  devised an audit system where they 'band' children
  according to level of support required and allocate
  funding accordingly).

■ there is additional resourcing for pupils with statements. This may be set down as a sum of money or in hours or support from a learning support assistant or teacher provided from LEA funding.

You need to find out (diplomatically) what funding is available to you and how it is used. Normally most of this money will be spent on staffing — including your post (although if you teach a full timetable this is more difficult to justify). According to the Code of Practice, the school's policy should state 'the allocation of resources to and amongst pupils with SEN' so that you need to know *what* the budget is and *how* it has been used and be able to propose a different form of allocation if you are not satisfied that the resources are being properly and efficiently used. Very often SENCOs have confused the SEN budget with their *capitation allowance* which allows you to buy materials and equipment for teaching pupils. Some schools may delegate this budget to you; in others you may have to make a request (with justification) for any purchase.

Your strategy for resource management must have a clear rationale and have been discussed and agreed with the headteacher, your colleagues and governors. The 'named' governor for SEN should be in a position to answer challenges from colleagues and parents, for any decision about resources will always be questioned and counter-proposals made. You must be able to justify your approach and demonstrate that you are monitoring its effectiveness. It is important, of course, not to become too rigid in applying your policy, as this could sometimes disadvantage an individual pupil. Nevertheless there should be a clear strategy related to the SEN policy.

Five steps in planning your resource allocation

1. Consider the target groups

■ pupils with statements
■ pupils at Stages 1–4 of the Code of Practice
■ all pupils (possibly including specific reference to the most able?)

You must be clear about how many pupils are at different stages and how they are distributed in different classes. The nature, severity and range of SEN must be considered.

2. The rationale for your allocation

What principles and criteria will underpin the use to be made of resources? (NB This question may be addressed fully, perhaps, only after taking steps 3–5).

3. An audit of available resources

■ *Human* — distinguish between support within the school and support from outside, e.g. Who are they? How are they used? Is there a financial implication?

	In School	**External**
Professional	Teachers Learning Support Assistants (LSAs)	Support services: Educational psychologists Specialist teachers/ non-teachers/SAs etc.
Voluntary	Pupils (e.g. peer tutors and 'buddy' systems; circle of friends, etc.)	Parents Other volunteers: governors Students/secondary schools/FE/Colleges/ HE

■ *Physical/material resources*:
— rooms/space (for teaching and/or resources)
— furniture (special tables, chairs, etc.)
— IT e.g. computer facilities (hardware/software)
— equipment, e.g. Braille reader, laptops, tape recorders, OHPs, video camera/recorder
— books, games, learning materials (published)
— teacher (or volunteer)-made materials

Managing people is considered in Chapter 3 and using LSAs in Chapter 10.

---

4. Time available

How much 'time' do you have from external/internal support teachers, assistants, other professionals?

5. Grouping for learning

Consider how pupils may be grouped for learning: use of small groups, individual work according to targets for pupils and nature of difficulties and support available. You should then be able to plan your strategy for making special educational provision in terms of resource allocation and negotiate appropriately with the headteacher, colleagues and governors. You will have to be able to justify your strategy in relation to the Code of Practice and, if necessary, convince others of your reasoning.

Managing material resources

A major part of your role will be to ensure that, within the limits of your capitation allowance, there are appropriate assessment and teaching materials available. There are implications for ordering, maintaining and storing resources for your colleagues who will appreciate not only knowledge about resources they could use to meet pupils' individual needs, but also easy access. A major task for many SEN coordinators is the management of teaching/learning resources such as special equipment, tapes, computers, software, books, games and other materials. Of course, even when you have established methods of collecting and cataloguing resources and set up a storage and borrowing system, there still remains the issue of ensuring they are used! You may have been in schools where resources lie untouched.

Choosing resources

Consultation with colleagues about the sort of resources they would like is useful, not only to try to give them a sense of ownership (with the aim of trying to make sure resources are used) but also because classroom teachers may bring a different perspective relating to curriculum access from yours which may be focusing on a narrower target related to a particular type of difficulty. Your SEN Adviser, other SENCOs, the SENCO forum, conferences, courses and professional journals are useful sources of guidance about materials. Publishers' catalogues and exhibitions are, of course, major sources of information about resources, but you need practical evaluation about their use.

When buying resources it is important to remember that as a coordinator you are accountable to the head and governors. You should:

- keep a copy of your order form and any purchase order/invoice;
- keep an inventory, with dates, of all stock;
- keep the inventory up to date and report lost/stolen/ destroyed stock;
- if you purchase equipment (such as computers) check the school's arrangements for security, insurance and *maintenance*;
- be aware of your responsibilities for maintenance and repair. Does the *school* pay or would any such costs come from your budget? (If the latter, you need to build this into your budget.)

Materials and equipment are very costly — particularly those relating to IT where, of course, there is very fast development with new, improved hardware and software appearing daily. The advice and support of your LEA ICT Adviser is essential. There are also several specialist SEN/IT companies and resource centres. The SENIT forum (on the Internet) enables you to request comments from other teachers and read results of earlier communications. When considering the costs of purchasing published materials you should make sure that the school's existing resources are fully used, and, if not, reconsider your potential purchases!

It is important to encourage colleagues to be prepared to share their resources, including not only commercially produced materials (some of which may be hidden, under-used, at the back of classroom cupboards), but also worksheets and materials which they may have produced themselves. Where this spirit of cooperation has been fostered, staff are often surprised by the quantity, quality and range of available resources.

Cataloguing and producing an index system (on cards and/or a computer database) are precursors to making resources accessible, and to identifying areas where further resources are required. Special schools, museum educational services and LEA support services may offer short-term loans/'trials' of materials, but sources for *supplementing* a school's resources are diminishing and very often schools must purchase or make their own materials. It is important here to be able to:

a) prioritise needs;

b) distinguish between materials which can be produced easily and to a professional standard by teachers and those where published materials both save time and are more attractive/'motivating' for pupils to use. Teachers can now produce materials to a high standard using IT and programmes like 'Worksheet Generator' (available from The Basic Skills Agency).

How to sort and catalogue materials

The most useful approaches appear to be to sort resources into the following categories:

1. *Assessment materials* — tests, methods for assessing a range of curriculum areas, basic skills and abilities which may underpin learning difficulties.

2. *Materials for teaching* which are related to specific difficulties (for example, to improve phonological awareness, to improve particular spelling skills, books for different reading age-levels).

3. *Cross-curricular teaching materials* (e.g. for teaching thinking, sequencing, listening skills, study skills).

4. *Equipment, aids and resources* such as computers, lap tops, concept keyboards, tape recorders (including 'low tech' e.g. triangular or 'pen-hold-grip' pen/pencil holders).

5. *Curriculum support* — materials not identified under 1, 2 and 3 above. There are two main approaches to this, with the first increasingly replacing the second. Resources are sorted into categories related either

   a) to the National Curriculum, e.g. schemes and materials to support English, science, maths, geography, etc.
      or
   b) to topic areas/the school's schemes of work, e.g. 'the Victorians', 'homes', etc.

6. *An SEN Information File* — this is a file (or set of files) containing information for your use or for consultation by the staff. (Some staff may prefer to refer to written material than ask for information.) Contents should include:

a) General information on a range of SEN/disabilities. There are 4 major sources:
   — materials from local support services
   — books/journals
   — leaflets from voluntary organisations (often specifically addressing school-related matters)
   — the Internet. There are a great many websites devoted to particular disabilities, and, of course, these are updated regularly. You could consider listing websites rather than storing paper copies you have downloaded. (This is an important source of information if, for example, you learn that a child has been diagnosed as having a particular syndrome which you have not previously encountered. You can download the information and circulate it to staff.) See Chapter 15 on using the Internet. The existence of these websites should mean a reduction in the size of this section of the file — you may wish to keep information only about the range of SEN most common in your school.

b) Information about local and national voluntary organisations to which you might need to refer parents. The basis for this must be a list of Voluntary Organisations which you can supply to parents (see Chapter 14). However, it is useful to supplement this list by providing the addresses, telephone numbers (and where possible contact names) of local groups. This is particularly useful where there might be parent support groups available. Such a list should be available from your LEA.

c) A list or directory of the support agencies (including voluntary organisations) which *you* can call on, together with the name of the local contact. It is useful here to note the range of advice/support available and to note the sort of information/detail they will require from you about any pupil. If you can prepare this prior to any telephone call or letter it can considerably reduce the time spent over the initial contact.

d) A list of publishers/suppliers of useful materials, together with current publicity, catalogue and price lists is invaluable.

Storage and retrieval

The following methods for storage/access to resources are those we have found in primary schools:

1. *A central resource base* — varying in size from a large classroom to a cupboard, the base provides central storage using clearly labelled trays, crates and files. Plastic wallets are used to store sets of materials where contents can easily be seen. Top copies of photocopiable materials are stored in plastic envelopes in ring-binders labelled according to subject matter. Copies of materials/worksheets most commonly used are stored in box files or filing cabinets. A 'logging' system is in operation for borrowing materials, including IT, software, overlays, etc. The key to this approach is that everything is 'in its place'.

2. *Resource trolleys* — this approach is similar to the above, but perhaps because of overall storage space, materials have been classified and sorted on to trolleys according to subject/area. The trolleys may be centrally stored or dispersed around the school. Staff must know both the location and materials available. A trolley (or more) can be taken to a particular classroom when required *or* materials borrowed from any trolley. A good 'logging' system is necessary. It is important to try to prevent 'sets' of materials being taken to a single classroom simply because a few items are required. The trolley system operates best if organised according to theme or subject.

3. *Resource files* — it may be useful to provide sources of information and copies of useful methods of assessments, teaching 'ideas' and a catalogue of the school's resources (and their locations) for *each* teacher, or make one or two copies to be kept in the staffroom for reference. These can be kept in box files or 'lever-arch' files/binders.

4. *Card index system* — this is a catalogue system, similar to the above, where a set of cards, based on one of the systems of categorisation suggested above, is stored centrally. This can contain information about:

> To help you to start your Resources File we have included a list of Voluntary Organisations and their addresses in Chapter 14.

— type of special educational needs
— assessment methods available
— teaching methods
— materials (purposes, uses)
— storage location

and include a 'signing out' system. A good system would allow (and encourage) users to add their own notes and teaching tips.

5. *Filing cabinet system* — this can be incorporated into a resource base/trolley approach and is a version of (4.) above. It combines an 'index' or cataloguing system with storage of worksheets and test materials. In particular this system has proved useful in primary schools where staff produce their own materials for copying. By filing them centrally they are available for wider use. Such a method engenders (and relies) on a collaborative staff!

Although cataloguing and sorting can take a long time, it may be possible to negotiate some time release for this (and we know of several primary schools where this has occurred) and to call on the services of parent volunteers to help with the actual labelling and sorting of materials, including setting up a data base on the computer.

We have found the following to be useful references on methods and approaches to teaching:

Gross, J. (1966) *Special Educational Needs in the Primary School: A Practical Guide* (*2nd ed*), Buckingham: Open University Press.

Pumfrey, P. (1991) *Improving Children's Reading in the Junior School: Challenges and Responses*, London: Cassell.

Westwood, P. (1997) *Commonsense Methods for Children with Special Needs* (*3rd ed*), London: Routledge.

Widlake, P. (1996) (ed.) *The Good Practice Guide In Special Educational Needs*, Birmingham: Questions Publishing.

Chapter 8

Managing the curriculum

Introduction

The Code of Practice implies that Individual Education Plans (IEPs) will help pupils to learn more effectively by targeting specific learning needs. However, for IEPs to do this, they must be developed within the context of the whole curriculum — which the Code does not address. In order to help children with SEN to learn more successfully, you have to consider the context of teaching and learning and all aspects of the curriculum — classroom organisation; grouping of pupils; curriculum content and delivery, including a teacher's style and *their* perceptions of teaching and learning. It is important to remember that the majority of children on the SEN Register will be taught by other teachers (not you!) and these teachers may have very different approaches to teaching — from each other and from you. As a SENCO you must be confident about a range of ways of managing teaching and learning which can offer support to teachers as well as learners.

Since the Education Reform Act (1988), all children have been entitled to a broad, balanced, relevant and differentiated curriculum, including the National Curriculum. Although procedures were put in place to allow for exemptions from or disapplication of the National Curriculum and associated assessments (either long-term or on a temporary basis) these do not seem to have been widely used. Under recent revisions (Dearing, 1994) the necessity for these formal procedures has been removed. Under former SCAA (School Curriculum and Assessment Authority) and now QCA (Qualifications and Curriculum Authority) direction, teachers may provide children with SEN programmes taken from an earlier key stage programme of study where appropriate. This, in itself, is a form of 'differentiation' of the curriculum. As matters concerning the National Curriculum and assessment have changed so often, you must make sure you keep up to date with any current requirements.

Curriculum entitlement

Curriculum entitlement should provide learning experiences which will ensure that all pupils, whatever their perceived ability, are challenged and helped where necessary and that their individual achievements are recognised and valued.

An entitlement curriculum implies inclusiveness and not a 'bolt on' set of activities for pupils with SEN. It implies the *participation* of pupils and not merely their presence in a classroom. This participation of all pupils must be reflected in both planning and in provision.

An entitlement curriculum should:

- promote development and progression
- provide learning experiences which ensure that all pupils, whatever their perceived ability are *challenged* and *helped* as necessary
- provide opportunities to recognise and value individual achievement
- be broad, balanced, relevant and differentiated

Components of the curriculum should enable pupils to:
- develop understanding of educational concepts and reflect on experiences in order to develop attitudes and values consistent with being a member of a modern society;
- acquire and develop knowledge across a range of subjects;
- have access to a variety of educational experiences and learning opportunities;
- develop a range of relevant skills, abilities and competences.

It is important to consider the extent to which all children will require access to the same knowledge, skills and experiences. Some pupils with SEN may need to learn certain prerequisite skills before they can participate in some areas of curriculum; some may need specific forms of training related to a disability (for example, mobility training for a blind child; signing for a child with severe hearing/communication difficulty). Where a child has a specific, 'exceptional' need then this should be identified, provided for and monitored through the IEP. In the case of most children with SEN, it is envisaged that the *majority* of their educational needs can be met in 'ordinary' classrooms through the provision of a differentiated curriculum, although *some* of their needs (where they may be at Stages 2–5 of the Code of Practice) will be met through a more specialised curriculum delivered either inside the classroom or on a withdrawal basis. The Code suggests that at Stage 1, the special educational needs are such that they can be met by the class teacher from within normal classroom provision. It this case the SEN are not significant and need no more than 'good mainstream teaching' which is differentiated to meet the normal range of abilities and attainments.

Differentiation

Differentiation is a process whereby planning and delivering the curriculum takes account of individual differences and matches what is taught and how it is taught to individual learning styles and needs. It seeks to provide opportunities for ALL children to participate and make progress in the curriculum by:

■ building on past achievement;
■ presenting challenges for further achievement;
■ providing opportunities for success.

Differentiation will involve teachers in:

■ assessing the current levels of functioning of pupils in subject areas and key skills;
■ determining the individual needs of pupils which may be expressed as learning objectives or intended learning outcomes;
■ selecting a range of methods of presenting tasks to pupils;

- being clear about their expectations of pupils and understanding how these may vary;
- accepting a range of different forms of evidence whereby pupils demonstrate what they know, understand or can achieve;
- adapting or modifying resources;
- varying the amount or nature of support given to pupils.

As a SENCO you will need to support some teachers in several of these aspects.

> **Differentiating the curriculum therefore can be said to be the process by which:**
>
> - curriculum aims and objectives
> - the stimuli and the input
> - the learning experiences and the content
> - teaching approaches and methods
> - resources and teaching aids
> - learning tasks and activities
> - assessment criteria and methods
> - the recording of what pupils know, understand and can do
>
> are all planned, modified, adapted or supported to meet the needs of individual pupils.

During any planning stage it is important that teachers build in how they will monitor progress through their record system and in relation to IEPs where a child is at Stages 2–5.

Monitoring pupils' progress is required for a range of purposes, including:

- providing feedback for pupils, parents and teachers and those who have been involved in the teaching of the pupil;
- providing evidence and performance indicators for school, the LEA, and other professionals who have a legitimate right to know;
- informing future planning and management of the education of the pupil;
- evaluating the approaches, methods and strategies which have been employed.

Helping colleagues to differentiate the curriculum is one of the major tasks of a SENCO, as it is so fundamental to primary teachers' abilities to meet SEN. The following overview of approaches to differentiation may provide a useful framework both for your own teaching and also to inform you if you are involved in providing staff development sessions for colleagues.

Models of differentiation

1. The 'Grouping for Learning' Model

This model includes various organisational methods of grouping pupils for learning. At the school level, the methods of banding, streaming or setting pupils tend to be used in secondary schools or in larger primary schools. It has been the practice on the whole for primary schools to use a variety of flexible grouping strategies *within* the classroom situation. These might include:

- friendship groups;
- ability groups within a particular programme of study;
- random groups;
- targeted groups;
- whole class teaching groups;
- individual activities.

It is important that the grouping of pupils is appropriate for the type of learning that is required and is consistent with the teaching and learning objectives identified by the teacher. Different types of learning can include:

- learning to develop or to improve an ability or a skill;
- learning to remember or recall knowledge or facts;
- learning to understand concepts;
- learning to develop attitudes and values.

A useful text is Dean (1987).

Depending upon the type of learning and the learning objectives, the teacher will need to consider which is the most appropriate grouping to achieve the learning.

2. The 'Must-Should-Could' Model

This involves a chain of tasks of progressive difficulty. At the 'must' level *all* students must complete the tasks and therefore they should be planned so that the least able pupils can achieve success. The teacher will need to ensure that pupils have the necessary prerequisite skills to carry out the early tasks. The 'must' level will tend to focus on core skills and knowledge.

The next level of difficulty will include some tasks and activities which *all* pupils have access to but not all pupils would be able to achieve *all* of the outcomes.

The highest level of difficulty will include tasks and activities which challenge the most able of pupils, but which are open to *all* pupils. The outcomes for some pupils might include the widening of experience and the raising of awareness. A useful source for information about this model is Brennan (1983).

3. The 'Core-Extension-Compensation/Consolidation' Model

This model, based upon that suggested by Lloyd-Jones (1985), involves setting a core of tasks for *all* pupils and then giving a range of tasks for pupils at either end of the ability/attainment continuum.

At the *Core* level, tasks are aimed at the development of key concepts and skills in relation to programmes of study and are accessible to all pupils.

At the *Extension* level, tasks are set at a more challenging level. This might include setting tasks which:
- are more open-ended;
- require the application of knowledge and skills in different situations;
- develop higher order skills, e.g. application, analysis, synthesis evaluation;
- require more research or investigation and require the pupil to develop a more a scholarly approach;
- require more detailed descriptions, more precise explanations and more sophisticated methods of recording;
- develop more creative thinking and more elaborate and more original responses.

At the *Compensatory* or *Consolidation* level, tasks are set in relation to individual needs. This might include setting tasks which focus on a small part of a scheme or programme of study:

- in small steps;
- using simplified language;
- using concrete materials;
- giving practical hands-on experience;
- using adapted resources;
- using multi-sensory resources;
- with a modified content;
- providing rehearsal or reinforcement activities;
- providing for support to complete tasks;
- employing particular teaching approaches or techniques;
- providing consolidation activities.

4. The 'Input/Process/Outcome' Model

This model adopts a process view of differentiating the curriculum and takes into account the individual differences pupils bring to the different learning situations, and the differences the different subject areas and types of learning require.

The individual differences which pupils bring to learning situations may include differences in:

- special educational needs
- learning styles
- learning rates
- prior learning experiences
- levels of functioning and attainment
- emotional and social needs

Different subject areas will require planning for learning at different levels in:

- concept acquisition
- the formation of attitudes and values
- knowledge acquisition
- the provision of experiences
- skills development
- cross-curricular themes

The 'Input/Process/Outcome' Model recognises that there are a variety of ways in which teaching and learning can be organised within the school or class, including:

- how learning is introduced and presented to pupils;
- what the learner is expected to do in order to learn;

- what the learning outcomes might be, how that learning is demonstrated, and how the teacher might respond to the learning.

This model proposes seven ways in which the curriculum may be differentiated:
- input
- task
- outcome
- output
- response
- resource
- support.

This model is particularly useful because it offers clear guidance to teachers.

Differentiation by input or introduction
Before planning a unit or scheme of work it is important to have an overview of:
— the key concepts, skills or knowledge which need to be developed;
— the prerequisite knowledge and skills in order to access the learning;
— any language demands which may cause problems;
— a common experience or interest which will make the learning relevant to the pupil.

Introducing the learning involves how the learning is presented to pupils and includes:
— range of stimuli;
— a starting activity;
— different modes, e.g. auditory/visual/motor;
— different teaching styles;
— a range of resources;
— different groupings;
— organising for different rates of learning.

Differentiation by task
This involves giving different groups of pupils tasks designed for different levels of ability or cognitive functioning. Tasks can be presented at different levels, which might include:

— the content to be presented;
— how the content or task is to be presented;
— what the pupils are expected to do;
— an individual pupil's role within the group.

Factors which will affect the difficulty of a task include:
— familiarity with the resources and materials;
— familiarity with the concepts and language;
— the number, density and complexity of the ideas, concepts and operations involved;
— the time allowed;
— the degree of support;
— the grading of the steps;
— the structuring within tasks.

Sharma (1990), for example, suggests that when planning mathematics lessons, teachers may need to include tasks which allow for:
— exploration;
— concrete experience;
— pictorial representation;
— symbolic representation;
— abstract conceptualisation;
— generalisation and application;
— communication of the learning.

Differentiation by outcome
This model is based on having different intended learning outcomes for pupils, related to a pupil's stage of development. It may well be that the learning experience or task is the same for all the pupils in a class, but what each pupil is expected to learn from the experience will vary according to individual levels of ability and need.

When learning is organised within the framework of differentiation by outcome, it is crucial that the teacher has identified *at the planning stage* where progression can be built in. It is also important that the intended learning outcomes or objectives are expressed in explicit, unambiguous language and, where appropriate, observable terms.

Teachers will need to consider how they will assess the learning outcomes and what evidence they will need to support their judgments. Assessment and supporting evidence

Setting precise learning objectives and targets will be discussed later in Chapter 9 when considering Individual Learning Programmes.

should take into account the range of individual differences and needs within the group. Teachers must be flexible in their expectations and take into account *unexpected* as well as *intended* learning outcomes. Teachers who only look for predetermined or expected outcomes may miss valuable evidence that pupils might provide regarding their learning. Techniques for assessing learning outcomes might include:

- observation
- questioning
- discussion
- listening
- assessment tasks.

Differentiation by output

This refers to how we ask or allow pupils to demonstrate what they know, understand and can do. There is always a concern that many pupils are prevented from recording their learning if they are restricted to written assignments. Sharma (1990) warned of the dangers of drawing conclusions about pupils' mathematical abilities, purely from their written tasks. Pupils, he reminds us, can achieve correct answers by using inefficient or faulty strategies. He suggests that we need to discover the processes and strategies pupils are using if we are to develop their abilities: it is only by observing them, talking to them and understanding their errors that we can truly assess their levels of mathematical thinking.

A range of methods of providing evidence of learning outcomes by output includes:

- annotated drawings
- diagrams
- worksheet with, e.g. multiple choice answers
- oral or taped responses
- participation in a debate or discussion
- artefact or model
- practical assignment, e.g. display
- participation in role play or drama.

Differentiation by response

This refers to how teachers respond and provide feedback to pupils' learning. Teachers should ask themselves if their marking policy provides meaningful feedback to themselves or to their pupils. Is the feedback meaningful to *all* pupils?

You might like to consider these questions in relation to your *own* practices for responding to pupils' work.
- Are the pupils involved in the target-setting and assessment procedures?
- Do teachers share the assessment and marking criteria with the pupils so that they know in advance what constitutes success?
- Are the assessment and recording procedures on-going and closely related to the teaching and learning processes and curriculum content?
- Do the marking and assessment procedures provide frequent, meaningful and constructive feedback to pupils?
- Do the reward systems reward effort as well as academic attainment?
- Does the system protect the self-esteem of pupils and reflect that pupils learn best in a climate in which they are happy and feel secure in their educational risk-taking?
- Do school systems include appropriate rewards and noteworthy recognition which develop the self-esteem of pupils and encourage them to take pride in their work and in their achievements?

Differentiation by resource

One of the most frequently used methods of ensuring accessibility to the curriculum is through the use of differentiated resources. This involves:

- ensuring the readability and understandability of the materials being used match those of the pupils;
- developing systems for the storage and retrieval of resources;
- ensuring that there is a wide range of resources available.

Supportive resources can include the use of:
- technology, including information and media technology
- audio and visual aids
- adapted, modified or simplified books and teaching materials
- the use of study guides
- resources-based learning
- supportive concrete materials.

The checklist in Figure 8.1 provides an overview of the factors which affect how children respond to texts.

Differentiation by support

One of the many ways in which teachers manage the teaching and learning of pupils is by the use of a range of support personnel. (Support can include a range of personnel, and the use of support teachers and support assistants is dealt with in Chapter 10.) In addition, teachers might:

- seek advice from specialist teachers;
- use range of volunteers in the classroom including parents;
- set up pupil support systems (either peer group support, using older pupils or students from local secondary schools).

FIG 8.1
Factors which affect suitability — readability

The reader
Age, Interest, Ability, Attitudes
Knowledge & Experience brought to the text
Language development and dialect
Cultural background
Reading skills and strategies
The physical, visual and auditory development of the pupil
The confidence of the pupil, fatigue; emotional state

Content
The conceptual difficulty; are the underlying ideas unusual or complex?
The familiarity of the reader with the content;
The relationship with other areas of the curriculum;
Is it fact or fiction;
The density of ideas per paragraph, page etc.
The interest of the content

Organisation
Does the text make it clear what the author is trying to do?
Is the information structured clearly and logically?
The sequencing of the information
Are the different elements or parts linked?
Does the author make use of summaries, diagrams, headings, sub-headings captions, etc.?
The relationship between the illustrations and the diagrams
The placement of the illustrations and the diagrams
The line length
Are there larger organisational features — contents page, glossary, index, bibliography?

The environment
Visibility; Seating position; Distraction; Level of noise

Language

Semantics:
The amount of information processing
The number of new content words — nouns — introduced and explained
How are different groups described
Cultural differences

Grammar/syntax:
Length of sentence
Difficult or unusual constructions
The genre and style of the writing: formal/informal language
Use of passive rather than active voice: an active verb rather than an
   abstract noun
The proximity of subject and verb
The number and use of stative verbs e.g. seems like, appears to, etc.
The frequency of pronouns
The proportion of connectives, linking words or phrases.
The number of clauses per sentence
The cohesiveness of the writing

Vocabulary:
Proportion of 'uncommon' words
Specialist or technical or formal words
The frequency of abstract nouns
Words introduced in unfamiliar contexts, e.g. coal-fields: Ambiguity

---

Layout/format/legibility
The use of illustrations and colour
Legible text with appropriate letter size, spacing, typeface and consistency
Spacing between the lines
Clearly laid out pages, good use of margins
Use of features, e.g. bold, underlining
The attractiveness of the material

Presentation
How the text is presented by the teacher
The purpose and nature of the task
What the learner is expected to do
The amount of time and the level of support provided

However, planning a varied curriculum and differentiating it to meet individual differences is, we maintain, fundamental to good primary practice, and indeed many teachers seem almost 'disappointed' when they find that there are no (or very few) specialist methods required.

Another way in which you can assist colleagues is to raise their awareness of a range of intervention strategies which have been used successfully with pupils with SEN. The following list, taken from Phillips and Cockett (1995), may be useful.

Suggestion

Audit of personal knowledge

Use the list of Intervention Strategies to assess your own knowledge and understanding. Identify any areas where you need to learn more before you could advise colleagues.

Suggestion

Consider the checklist provided on p. 141 for evaluation how well lessons meet individual needs. Use it and your own ideas to provide a sheet for colleagues to use to evaluate their own lessons in terms of meeting SEN.

There are many aspects of where improving learning experiences for children with SEN has improved the educational opportunities for all children. We would specifically point to the benefits of:

- teaching thinking and problem-solving skills;
- teaching study skills;
- teaching pupils how to learn independently;
- using IT;
- improving the use of questioning techniques during teaching;
- positive teaching in raising self-esteem.

As a SENCO you will be well aware of the effects of learning difficulties on children's self-esteem. Very often there may be associated emotional and behavioural difficulties where you may have to support both staff and children. It is important that any discussion of the curriculum (including the 'hidden' curriculum) pays attention to the affective side of children's development and education as well as the cognitive and academic. Although there is heightened awareness that a large (and apparently rising) number of children at primary schools are presenting behaviour difficulties, very often a response has been to suspend or exclude them, resulting in a growing number of primary-aged children who are 'disaffected' and taking 'unauthorised absences'.

For many, the reasons for learning difficulties may include curriculum-related factors. A SENCO can be influential in affecting teachers' attitudes towards such children as well as helping them to devise individual programmes to improve behaviour and target learning objectives. One major, powerful source of influence will be that where teachers provide a more appropriate curriculum and supportive classroom, pupils will learn more successfully and be less likely to 'reject' school. Their behaviours and attendance should improve.

Chapter 9

Developing individual learning: IEPs and ILPs

Introduction

Individual Education Plans (IEP) are required from Stage 2 of the Code of Practice and as SENCO you will normally be involved in helping staff to develop them, perhaps advising them on their implementation and monitoring, and bearing responsibility for monitoring and review. Developing and monitoring a child's IEP is a major aspect of the role of a SENCO, and an IEP often reveals the strengths (and weaknesses) of a school's policy, procedures and coordination of SEN.

The Code of Practice suggests that an IEP at Stage 2 should set out:
- the nature of the child's learning difficulties;
- action
  - the special educational provision;
  - staff involved, including frequency of support;
  - specific programmes/activities/materials/equipment;
- help from parents at home;
- targets to be achieved in a given time;
- any pastoral care or medical requirements;
- monitoring and assessment arrangements;
- review arrangements and date.

You should refer back to Chapter 5 for some of the implications for procedures.

As far as possible, provision should be made in the normal classroom setting and, therefore, the plan should be related to the curriculum followed by the class and should refer to programmes and materials which are readily available to a child's class teacher. At Stage 3 the only difference is in the 'action' section on special educational provision which should specify;

- school staff involved, including frequency and timing of support;
- external specialist involved, including frequency and timing;
- specific programmes/activities/materials/equipment.

In other words the support not normally available from within the school's own resources should be made explicit (and it is the need for this which is related to proposing that a child is at Stage 3).

Individual Education Plan or Individual Learning Programme?

In some schools there is a single, very specific IEP whereas in others, the IEP is regarded more as the long-term *strategy* and more detailed specific individualised learning programmes are drawn up to help teachers or learning support assistants to teach and monitor progress on a more day-to-day basis. The term Individual Learning Programme (ILP) is often used to distinguish between the two. It is important to remember that whereas schools should develop IEPs under the Code of Practice, an ILP is discretionary and merely one way of planning teaching.

It is important to review the IEPs in use in your school and obtain staff opinions about their usefulness, including the format. A SENCO should always work with a class teacher in drawing up an IEP for a child, and this not only ensures that the teacher feels responsible for the IEP but also provides an opportunity for 'incidental' professional development. Very often, through collaborative planning, teachers extend their knowledge, skills and understanding of SEN more than through more formal inservice activities, because there is immediate relevance to their practice.

In writing an IEP there should be clear targets. These will usually relate to assessment of needs in one or more of the following areas:

General	Health Physical Development/Functioning Attendance, Punctuality, etc.
Motor/sensory	Mobility, Gross Motor Skills, Fine Motor Skills, Auditory–Visual Perceptual Development, etc.
Communication	Receptive Language Development, Expressive Language Development Speaking, Listening, etc.
Personal/social/ emotional	Interests, Self-esteem, Independence, Interpersonal Skills, Emotional Development, Behaviour, etc.
Educational	Cognitive Functioning, Concept Acquisition, Literacy, Numeracy, Generalisation, Approaches and Attitudes to Learning, Learning Styles: Educational Attainments (including National Curriculum levels)
Other	Any other areas which are deemed appropriate.

Colleagues should be encouraged to use the above to build up a profile of the pupil, using teacher judgments supported by assessments.

Making judgments

Drawing up a profile will involve making judgments as to whether:

- the pupil's level of competence and need is consistent with those of pupils of the same age;
- the pupil has additional or special needs in this area;
- the pupil has a particular strength in this area.

To provide a perspective on the frequency or severity of a particular difficulty or behaviour, it is useful to consider a continuum and to place the particular behaviour along it. Teachers may find it useful to consider describing the

- *frequency* in terms of Never, Rarely, Occasionally, Frequently, Usually, Always;
- *severity* in terms of Mild, Moderate or Severe;

- *timescale* in terms of Temporary or Long-term;
- *level of competence* in terms of Cannot attempt, With support, Independently;
- *level of mastery* in terms of: Has had experience of, Working on, Mastered.

When the areas of concern have been identified and priorities have been decided upon, the next step is to identify the pupil's baseline in learning or behaviour.

Target setting

A useful approach to target setting is to encourage colleagues to express their objectives as SMART targets. That is, they should be

Specific

Measurable

Achievable

Relevant

Timed (i.e. have a timescale for review)

Thus the IEP should state:
- what the SMART target is;
- what objectives will be set to achieve the target;
- how and when the target will be achieved.

For example, consider a child in Year 6 with particular reading difficulties where the IEP will be reviewed at least after 6 months and possibly termly. Currently the child has a Reading Age of 6.3 yet is nearly 11 years old. The IEP should state:
- What the Smart *target* is

  e.g. to achieve a Reading Accuracy Age of 8 using a new Neale Analysis.
- What the objectives will be towards achieving this target, based on existing strengths and weaknesses

  e.g. a) to read CVVC words correctly (e.g. seek)

  b) to read CVCV (where final V is 'e', e.g. cake, correctly).
- How and when the target will be achieved

  e.g. a) session of 15 minutes in-class support daily from a Learning Support Assistant (LSA) using 'Alpha to Omega';

Issues of monitoring and reviewing IEPs are considered in Chapter 5.

b) word-recognition reading game used at home twice a week with parent;

c) once-a-week use of computer programme to reinforce the above, (supervised by the LSA).

Resources, length of period, venue and personnel should be identified. (In addition, of course, the other aspects of an IEP should also be stated.)

All the terms used in the IEP should be clear and understood by everyone concerned. In the above account, the SENCO should explain what 'Reading Accuracy' means and give examples and explanations of CVVC and CVCV (final 'e') words to parents. The SENCO has responsibility for coordinating and monitoring the provision but, unless the IEP is for a child in the SENCO's own class, delivery will be by others.

An example of the format of an IEP used by some schools is provided Figure 9.1 on (see pp. 150–51). Compare this with that used in your own school, and with the ILP format in Figure 9.2 on p. 155.

Individual Learning Programmes (ILP)

An ILP is often drawn up in order to specify the steps and the teaching requirements to enable an individual pupil to meet a specific target. It is worthwhile for you to help colleagues understand the difference between the IEP, which identifies and sets out how a set of prioritised needs are going to be met and the parts different people involved will play, and an ILP, which is a structured teaching programme which sets out how any one of the targets might be met. The target objective of a particular ILP will have a specified timescale which will be dependant on the identified need.

An ILP has its origins in behavioural psychology and the 'teaching to objectives' approach. Some teachers may be concerned about this kind of approach in terms of its precision and the decontextualised manner in which it may be carried out. There may be concerns that pupils could be required to move through small steps without understanding the basic

Individual Education Plan: Stage 2

Name of pupil:_____ Form/class _____

Date of birth:_____ C.A. _____ Home language _____

Date IEP agreed _____ Review date _____

Is this the first or second IEP at Stage 2 | 1 | 2 |

Reasons why special provision is being made:

Objectives/targets to be Achieved

Action to be taken	Who is involved	Any special resources

Summary of pupil's contribution.

Individual Education Plan: Stage 2 continued

Summary of parents/carers' involvement

Special arrangements for curricular access

Non curricular needs

Monitoring arrangements and responsibilities:

First review _____ Date _____

Outcomes and action:

Parents notified (if not present) _____

Second review date (if applicable) _____

Who is responsible for this? _____

If new Individual Education Plan at Stage 2 is proposed please note here, including:

Date of new IEP at Stage 2 _____

Date of second review (Stage 2) _____

© The Manchester Metropolitan University, Didsbury School of Education

From: *Special Educational Needs: Putting the Code to Work*

FIG 9.1
Example of an IEP

> Setting clear targets should not imply that teaching becomes boring and mechanical.

underlying concepts or without seeing the relevance to the overall aims of the IEP and to their learning. It is important, therefore, that this kind of structured approach is used *only* when it is appropriate in meeting a pupil's individual needs, that all involved can see the apparent purpose and the relevance, and that the teaching of the steps is carried out in an interesting and motivating way. In other words, the sort of detailed approach described here may not be necessary for all pupils. Moreover the use of an ILP should normally be seen as only one aspect of the child's curriculum and there is an expectation that the pupil will follow the normal curriculum of the rest of the class wherever possible, with appropriate differentiation strategies and/or support made available as detailed on the IEP. Indeed such approaches may be used when a child needs to learn skills to facilitate curriculum access. It is important, therefore, to ensure that the pupil is encouraged to use and practise these new skills within their normal curriculum activities. An ILP will also involve ongoing assessment and record keeping and it is essential that the pupil is given frequent feedback and participates in the target setting and recording of progress.

Identifying learning objectives

Detailed diagnostic assessment (including using observation) will be necessary to discover precisely where the pupil is experiencing difficulties, to find 'gaps' in knowledge or skills and define the pupil's strengths in relation to these difficulties. In this way it will be possible to identify the next 'step' towards achieving the overall target. To distinguish between this first step and the overall target identified on the IEP we have used the term 'objective', but it is worth noting that some writers and schools may use the word target for both.

The first objective towards any target should represent a challenge, so that there must be consideration of what is known about the pupil's rate of learning before deciding on both the size of the step and timescale. You will need to ask if there are any issues which might affect the achievement of the objective. These might include identifying any techniques or resources which have proved to be particularly effective or which the pupil particularly likes and, similarly, discovering whether any techniques or resources have proved to be particularly unsuccessful.

Delivering the teaching associated with an ILP has implications for the efficient use of time for the pupil and the teacher or support assistant. Careful planning, involving the identification of appropriate steps and the most effective strategies and resources, is crucial. It is also important not to waste time on what the pupil can already do. 'The next step' should always take the pupil forward. However, the teaching programme will need to build into the framework frequent opportunities to consolidate or reinforce learning.

Once the next step to be achieved has been identified, the specific learning objective should be expressed in unambiguous, explicit and, where possible, observable terms. Some teachers involved in developing or monitoring ILP for pupils adopt a behavioural approach and require the target (or objectives) to include three components:

1. *A clear and unambiguous description of what the pupil should be able to do at the end of the teaching process.* This is often expressed in behavioural terms so that it can be observed and, therefore, will include a verb to describe the action. Some examples are given below:
   - Name of pupil, followed by:
     - will **name** familiar objects
     - will **write** own name correctly
     - will **read** and write lower case letters
     - will **read** phonetically regular 3 letter words
     - will **give** change from £1
     - will **tell** time
     - will **stay** on task

2. *The conditions under which the action should be performed.* These could include a description of the materials to be used or a description of how the task is to be presented, for example:
   - will read **from a list** . . .
   - will copy **from a model placed directly above** . . .
   - will write **without support** . . .
   - **using apparatus**, will solve simple written problems involving numbers up to 20.
   - will join in conversation **initiated by the teacher and other children**.

3. *The criteria which will indicate success.* It can specify a level of success required and/or the number of occasions the pupil is required to provide evidence of success, for example:

— will put on coat **in two minutes**

— will count to 100 hundred **without error**

— will bring specified equipment to school **on 4 days out of 5**

— will read specified key words **without error on six consecutive occasions**

How to decide on 'the next step'

Many teachers become concerned about how to break down a target into small steps in a sequence. Some feel anxious because they believe there is perhaps a specific, preordained, incremental sequence to particular learning behaviours (for example, in handwriting or reading). In most cases, whilst it *is* possible to analyse many learning tasks and activities, there is no single 'correct' approach. However, consultation between colleagues, particularly subject specialists and teachers with understanding of learning difficulties can provide useful structures for SENCOs and class teachers to use in isolating, sequencing and describing steps in performance terms.

Several resources are also available to help, such as baseline assessment schemes, the National Literacy Strategy and small steps programmes. It is important to remember that, in some cases, the sequence of steps is significant, but not in others. It is equally important not to make steps so small and so many that the overall target is forgotten.

Teaching strategies and resources

Attention needs to be given to selecting methods and resources which have proved successful with a particular pupil. The expertise of learning support services and subject coordinators within the school will be useful. The approaches and materials to be used should be identified on the child's ILP so that where a child learns particularly quickly (or the reverse) it is possible to consider the contribution of the methods used. See Figure 9.2 for an example of how to select and record teaching activities with a particular child.

NAME:.................................. STAGE.......................... ILP NO:........................ TARGET OBJECTIVE:.......................

Date & Step (Behaviour Conditions)	Date: Teaching Activity: Resources	COMMENT

© Falmer Press

FIG 9.2
Individual learning programme: Teaching activities

INDIVIDUAL LEARNING PROGRAMME (ILP1)

NAME:.. STAGE:..

DATE OF ILP:... ILP NO...

TARGET AREA...

OVERALL OBJECTIVES OF ILP (Pupil Behaviour/Conditions/Criteria)

STEPS		DATE STARTED	DATE MASTERED	DATE CHECKED

Comment on Progress: DATE:

FIG 9.3
Example of an ILP

© Falmer Press

Monitoring and recording progress

As part of the process of developing ILPs, the SENCO and support staff will need to decide on how the children are to be monitored and their progress recorded. Examples of such a record (reduced in size) is provided in Figure 9.3. The record should include the date the ILP was started and when the target objective has been mastered. As well as the teacher record, it is also beneficial if the pupil can be involved in the recording of progress. Again there are some useful commercially produced recording sheets, although many schools make use of their IT expertise and facilities to develop their own.

Remember, that the assessment of the learning objective should be consistent with the teaching approach of that objective. If it appears that the learning objective is not being achieved then teachers will need to consider the possible reasons. It may be that the teaching approach or resources should be changed, or even the objective. This may mean breaking the target into smaller steps or selecting another target associated with the area of concern, perhaps returning the original one later.

As part of the process, *maintenance* and *generalisation* will need to be built in. Maintenance (being able to perform a skill accurately and fluently after a period of time) and generalisation (being able to apply the knowledge and skill in different contexts) means that the target objectives will need to be revisited from time to time and activities designed to enable the pupil to apply the acquired knowledge and skill.

As SENCO, you might well be involved in drawing up an ILP but will rarely be involved in delivering it. In most schools, the teaching and monitoring is carried out by a class teacher, a Support Teacher (usually part-time) or Learning Support Assistant (full or part-time). Anyone who is involved in developing, teaching and monitoring an ILP should fully understand the rationale, overall target and processes involved.

You might like to complete the following activity for a pupil known to you.

Suggestion

Deciding whether to use ILPs and IEPs

List the advantages and disadvantages of using ILP from a pupil's and teacher's viewpoint

	Advantages	Disadvantages
P U P I L		
T E A C H E R		

Part three | Working with others

Chapter 10

Managing support

A major aspect of the SENCO's role is to manage the support systems for meeting SEN. Supporting teaching and learning is fundamental to the development of inclusive education where it becomes part of a whole-school approach to curriculum management and staffing policies rather than a means of meeting the needs of a small number of pupils. You need to be conscious of the position of SENCOs as potential agents for change in the philosophy and practices identified in the Green Paper *Excellence for All Children* (DfEE, 1997b). Your role is to ensure that the primary school can effectively meet the needs of *all* children, not to think of 'support' as something required by a few children in order to 'maintain' them in a mainstream school.

There are two major aspects to your role in managing and organising support:
1. Your own involvement in providing direct support.
2. Your management of others engaged in providing and receiving support.

I. The support role of the SENCO

A SENCO is directly involved in providing support in the following ways:

Suggestion

Personal Reflection

- What do you see as the main purposes of 'support' in a school?
- To what extent to you agree that 'learning support' may be a way of 'labelling children and not changing school systems and curriculum'?

- consultancy and advice to colleagues on identifying, assessing and providing for the needs of individual children;
- consultancy and counselling for parents;
- direct teaching of individual children/small groups;
- support within and outside classes, particularly where there is some non-contact time (i.e. where you are not teaching a class full time). This sort of direct support by a SENCO in another teacher's classroom is, unfortunately, rare in primary schools because the SENCO normally has responsibility for a class.

2. Managing support staff and strategies

SENCOs often have responsibility for managing the work of Learning Support Teachers (LST) employed by the school (often on a part-time basis), Learning Support Assistants (LSA) employed by the school and/or LEA (full or part-time), and coordinating the support offered by external agencies. This part of provision, although it must be fully integrated within the school's procedures, as described in Chapter 5, is dealt with in a later chapter.

Responsibility for learning support teachers and assistants has implications for:

- managing and organising (calling on all the skills described in the first four chapters of this book);
- selecting appropriate support methods (requiring decision-making and leadership skills);
- interviewing and drawing up job descriptions;
- training and staff development (of supporters and *all* staff).

Who provides support?

Support for pupils with SEN may be provided by a range of different people with a range of different specialisms and qualifications. These may include:

Teachers

Provider	Support	Qualification/Status
School	Special Educational Needs Coordinator (SENCO)	Qualified teacher May have additional general SEN and/or specialist qualifications
	Support Teacher	Qualified Teacher May have additional general SEN and/or specialist qualifications
LEA	Specialist Support Teacher	Qualified Teacher May have additional general SEN and/or specialist qualifications for particular area of SEN.
Special School	Outreach Teacher	Qualified Teacher May have additional general SEN and/or specialist qualifications for particular area of SEN

Support assistants

Provider	Support	Qualification/Status
School	Classroom Assistants (CA) Support Assistants (SA) Nursery Nurses Non-Teaching Assistants (NTA)	May have: ■ an NNEB qualification ■ a general SEN qualification ■ other formal qualification ■ no qualification or training
LEA	Special Support Assistant	May have: ■ an NNEB qualification ■ a general SEN qualification ■ other formal qualification ■ no qualification or formal training
School	Parent Volunteers	May have: ■ some qualification and training ■ no qualification or training
	Pupil support Peer Tutors	

A range of other professionals may be involved and these are discussed in Chapter 12.

Hart (1986) noted that many of the debates regarding support have been tied up with the location of the support — i.e. 'In-class support' and 'Withdrawal support' — rather than the nature or the precise purpose of the support. The activity above asked you to reflect on the purpose of support. Although most teachers would argue that the purpose of support is to support children with special educational needs, it may be possible to differentiate between:

- support for individual pupils, aimed particularly at supporting their IEP;
- curriculum support which includes methods to enable all pupils to access, participate in and derive benefit from learning;
- emotional support for both pupils and staff.

You can see from this that the majority of your activities involve all forms of offering 'support'.

Postlethwaite and Hackney (1988) identify three levels of support strategies used by schools:

Level 1. **Consultancy advice** on how to identify or respond to the needs of individual children causing concern or identified at Stage 2 of the Code of Practice. This would be in addition to general professional development and advice on strategies for differentiating the curriculum, programmes of study and resources covered in school-based INSET days.

Level 2. **In-class support** for some pupils for specific lessons or for specific amounts of time on a long term or short term basis depending upon the purpose.

Level 3. **Withdrawal periods** for some pupils for differing amounts of time for differing purposes.

Throughout the book, reference has been made to your role as consultant to staff. It is important to offer advice as a colleague not 'expert', using the interpersonal skills identified earlier. Whilst advice is required at all Stages of the Code of Practice, it is a particularly sensitive issue at Stage 1 where a teacher is responsible for meeting a child's needs without necessarily any specific direct intervention from the SENCO or external support teacher.

Advice at Stage 1 might include:

- helping to agree upon criteria for the identification of SEN in the classroom
- confirming the teacher's judgment that there is a legitimate cause for concern
- informing the teacher about the educational or personal/social implications of pupil's identified difficulty
- helping the teacher to develop a wider range of identification, diagnostic or teaching strategies
- helping the teacher to develop more preventative approaches to learning or behaviour difficulties, e.g. analysing classroom organisation as a possible cause of difficulties
- teaching tips, e.g. for an identified need such as a handwriting problem or minor behaviour difficulty
- developing, modifying or adapting teaching resources for class teachers to use with particular children.

Clearly one of the main problems with support at Stage 1 is the lack of time for effective consultations. Some schools, however, in an effort to overcome this difficulty, allocate staff meetings/or part of staff meeting time to discuss 'pupils causing concern'.

We must not under-estimate the value and the importance of class teachers meeting the needs of their pupils supported by the advice of colleagues. Teachers have always been best-placed to meet the needs of most of their pupils and only in exceptional cases has it been necessary to provide for those needs from other sources. It is essential, therefore, that teachers are continually updated with ideas and strategies. Summarising their findings regarding mainstream teachers' views about this type and level of support, Postlethwaite and Hackney (1988) commented that:

> ❝ ... *advice to mainstream staff can be a powerful and all-pervasive element in the special needs support system of a school. It should certainly not be ignored, a mainstream teacher may be the only source of support for some special needs children (e.g. those with needs which are temporary and for which there is not time for other support services to be deployed), and will be the main form of support for others whose needs are sufficiently mild that any other support is available for only a small part of the week.* (Postlethwaite and Hackney, 1988, p. 61)

This first stage of meeting SEN should be recognised as crucial to a whole-school graduated response or continuum of provision.

A major concern of SENCOs regarding this first level of support is the 'bureaucracy' or perceived amount of 'unnecessary paperwork' which will not necessarily result in any more direct support for the pupil. This could be a prohibiting factor in teachers identifying and meeting the needs of pupils SEN at Stage 1. It is important, therefore, that your advice emphasises to them their own skills in differentiation and the need only to monitor progress. There should not be a great deal of 'paperwork' at this stage.

There is also a concern that for various reasons some teachers may receive advice, but will not necessarily act upon it. You must call on interpersonal strategies here, but, in the event of failure to negotiate appropriate action, you may have to seek intervention from the headteacher.

A model for educational support for SEN

It is possible to draw up a support model which addresses the concerns of 'purpose' in relation to location (see Figure 10.1).

In-class support or withdrawal?

The debates about the most effective and efficient use of support staff continue, including arguments about whether children should be given in-class support or withdrawn from lessons for intensive teaching related to their particular difficulties. Where the support they require is highly specialist, individualised and not directly related to the normal primary curriculum (for example, sessions from a physiotherapist or speech therapist), then there is considerable agreement that this is best met outside the classroom. However, the issue of support for *learning* is less straightforward.

The main arguments **against** withdrawal are:
- expensive use of teachers/learning support staff because they work with only one or a small group of pupils;
- there is no impetus to making changes in the curriculum so that it meets the child's needs (yet most of a child's time will be spent *in* that classroom);

FIG 10.1
A model for educational support
for SEN

SUPPORTING ILP (TARGETED SUPPORT)	CURRICULUM ACCESS SUPPORT
Development and Planning Developing, planning and preparing resources to support the IEP outside classroom	**Development and Planning** Preparing, planning, modifying or adapting curriculum materials outside classroom
Direct support 2. Supporting pupils in a 1–1 situation outside the classroom (withdrawn/extracted from class)	*Direct support* 2. Supporting pupils in a 1–1 situation outside the classroom — withdrawn from the subject area. Following: a) Programme of Study (POS) b) a modified POS or c) an adapted POS
3. Supporting pupils 1–1 in the classroom following a special programme	3. Supporting pupils in a 1–1 situation in class. Following: a) Programme of Study (POS) b) a modified POS or c) an adapted POS
4. Supporting pupils in a small group (SG) situation outside the class following a special programme	4. Supporting pupils in a SG outside the class (withdrawn) following: a) Programme of Study (POS) b) a modified POS or c) an adapted POS
5. Supporting pupils in a SG situation in the classroom on a special programme	5. Supporting pupils in a SG in class following: a) Programme of Study (POS) b) a modified POS or c) an adapted POS
The individual or special learning programme can involve: ■ developing literacy and numeracy skills ■ a behaviour programme ■ a therapeutic, care or social programme ■ supporting learning to operate specialised or technical equipment ■ homework support	6. Supporting all pupils who need help in the classroom meeting needs as they arise
	7. Working in a partnership or a team arrangement with the class or subject teacher
	Curriculum support can also involve acting as: scribe, interpreter, reader organiser, providing attention and reinforcement pre- and post-teaching

- it 'mystifies' what happens in special education rather than empowering and enskilling classroom teachers;
- possible negative effects on a pupil's self-esteem because they are seen as 'special';
- the pupils may come to be too dependent on support;
- it results in children losing part of the mainstream curriculum;
- very little evidence of long-term effects.

The same arguments can also be made, of course, when a teacher gives support *within* a class, but only to one or a small group of pupils, and what has developed over the last 15–20 years is a wide range of strategies for supporting pupils within classrooms (and outside) which extend learning opportunities for greater numbers of children and contribute towards changes in the curriculum. Thus such methods not only help pupils access the curriculum, but lead to curriculum development and enhance teachers' professional development.

TYPES OF SUPPORT	

In-class
 can involve:
 ■ support for individuals and small groups within the class
 ■ the supporter meeting needs as they arise from any pupil not just SEN
 ■ providing more attention and immediate reinforcement for particular pupils
 ■ both teachers proving staff development for each other (discussing ideas)
 ■ co-teaching as a means of curriculum development
 ■ a partnership arrangement involving joint planning, teaching, recording and assessment (teach part lesson)
 ■ maximising the range of approaches to teaching
 ■ developing resources
 ■ opportunities to extend and challenge very able pupils as well as those with difficulties
 (n.b. A pupil's curriculum entitlement will be protected. If a child is removed, even for a short time, parents should be informed.)
	Out-of-class
	 can involve:
	 a) ■ the Learning Support Teacher (LST) developing resources for class teacher (CT)
	   ■ joint planning (LST & CT) but only CT teaches
	 b) ■ individual learning programmes for short-term intensive periods, e.g. in areas of weakness or to achieve specific targets: this is usually employed to remove a barrier to learning or to develop a coping skill
	   ■ special/or alternative curriculum for, e.g., exceptionally able or disaffected pupils or for pupils with great difficulties (used sparingly and sensitively)
	   ■ arrangements for pupils who have missed work
	   ■ pre-and/or post-teaching
	   ■ arrangements to provide consolidation activities
	   ■ resource-based activities, e.g. flexible learning programmes: special projects
	   ■ provision for pupils with social and emotional difficulties
	   ■ arrangements for pupils who will respond better for a particular programme away from distractions
	 c) ■ help with organising homework programmes
	   a) forms of curriculum development
	   b) forms of tutorial support
	   c) homework support

In order to support pupils' access to the curriculum, some schools prefer to utilise their support staff in the preparation of appropriate resources by modifying or adapting materials or by designing more appropriate resources for particular pupils.

Tutorial or Individual support should be considered for specific target objectives with a specified timescale. This type of support will be provided in response to identified needs and as an outcome of an action planning meeting where the precise learning targets, the teaching requirements, and the monitoring and reviewing arrangements will have been made explicit.

The pupil's National Curriculum entitlement must be protected and parents should be consulted with regard to any exceptional arrangements that are being made for a particular pupil.

Different types of in-class support

In-class support to facilitate curriculum access can take various forms. The following descriptions include some of the types used in schools.

Type of support	Features
Cooperative or partnership teaching	■ Both teachers share responsibility for planning, preparation, delivery of lessons, supporting pupils, monitoring, assessment and recording. ■ Both teachers have equal status. ■ Planning and evaluation are crucial and time is allocated to this. ■ The curriculum is planned with SEN in mind and differentiation is built in from the beginning. ■ The more individual needs are taken into account, the less special provision needs to be made. ■ Good practice and new ideas are shared. ■ It is possible to offer a wider range of teaching and learning styles and activities. ■ The process setting learning goals, teaching, evaluating, reviewing, disseminating. ■ Pupils can be involved in the process.
Providing support	This can include the above but does not necessarily do so. ■ It can involve adapting or modifying or supporting tasks without being involved in the planning. ■ It can involve a range of adults not just teachers. ■ Support can be provided for one pupil, a small group of pupil or any pupil needing help. ■ The manner in which the support is utilised can vary according to the number of adults available, their skills and abilities, the number of pupils requiring support. Roles and tasks need to be clarified in advance to avoid negative outcomes (this will be developed a little more fully later).

To illustrate the types of support which might be offered in the classroom situation the following might be considered. Often a combination of the roles is used depending on the particular situation regarding the pupils' needs and the skills and time available at the time.

In-class support	Models of working
Free-wheeling/floating	■ The supporter moves around the room and offers support to any pupil in the class who requires it.
Class consultant	■ The supporter sits at a desk and can be consulted by any pupil seeking help.
Dialogue role	■ The class teacher and the support teacher enter into a dialogue to explain, e.g., concepts.
	■ The supporter may be seen as 'interpreter'.
Summariser	■ The supporter summarises key points in a lesson.
Special teacher/supporter	■ Support is offered to identified pupil/pupils who may or may not sit together.
Special class/group teacher	■ Identified pupils sit together and are taught by the support teacher or support assistant (lesson within a lesson).
	■ The materials and resources used may be the same as or different from those used by the rest of the class.

Suggestion

Choosing support strategies

Consider the learning support staff (teachers/assistants) for which you have responsibility.

1. Using the models and strategies outlined in this chapter list their current ways of working and state what purposes they serve.

2. What changes, if any, would you wish to see?

3. Draw up a plan of the support strategies you wish to see and develop for your school using the headings of: Role (LSA or LST), type of support, Hours/week, Class/Subject/Pupils. Specify how they would work and to what purpose.

Hart (1986) identified the importance of having the purpose and the exact nature of the support clarified and understood by all concerned, together with the objectives, the tasks and responsibilities associated with the support specified in advance. If the purpose, the nature, the tasks and responsibilities are not clarified in advance the following can occur:

■ The supporter can find him/herself standing on the sideline for long periods of time, for example, while the teacher is introducing the main concepts to the class.

■ The supporter can find him/herself helping pupils to complete tasks which are unsuitable and inappropriate.

■ There is nothing to do while the pupil is completing tasks.

■ Pupils may feel stigmatised by having attention drawn to them.

■ Pupils may feel confused as to how to treat the supporter.

In-class support: Areas for clarification

Experience has shown that it is useful for the class teacher and the support teacher to meet to discuss certain areas, in order to avoid misunderstandings later on. The following set of questions may be helpful as a checklist or a set of guidelines for teachers working together:

1. What are the aims of this method of working?
2. Is the present classroom organisation suitable for cooperative teaching?
3. How do the personalities of the two teachers working together combine?
4. Will there be any time for planning, reviewing, evaluation? How often will they need to meet?
5. Who will do the preparation, presentation and marking of work?
   Will the support teacher take the lead in the presentation of any lessons?
6. What arrangements are in place, if one teacher is away?
7. Is it necessary to explain any of the arrangements to the pupils?
8. Is the support teacher there to help particular children or the whole class?
9. Who has overall responsibility for any discipline problems?
   How can one teacher intervene without undermining the authority of the other?
   Have both teachers a consistent view regarding behaviour and discipline?
10. Will the perceived status of the teachers outside the classroom present difficulties?
    How can it be ensured that both teachers are perceived by the pupils as being of equal status in the classroom?
11. How will responsibility for assessment be shared?
12. What arrangements are there for report writing and parents' evenings?
13. Will the classroom support be instead of or in addition to any withdrawal sessions?
14. What will the support teachers do while the pupils are working independently on tasks?
15. Have both teachers a consistent view on the teaching of subjects, e.g. literacy?

> Many of these questions can be applied equally when a teacher is supported by a Classroom or Learning Support Assistant

16. Do both adults have a consistent interpretation of the classroom rules and routines?

Working with learning support assistants

There is a growing tendency to make use of a range of types of support assistant to support the needs of pupils within all stages of the Code of Practice. Some are directly employed by schools as part of the school-based stages of provision. Others are employed by the LEA and form part of the support provided within the 'statement of provision'.

These support assistants may be referred to as Special Support Assistants (SSA), Special Needs Assistants (SNA), Classroom Assistants (CA), and, in some cases, Non-Teaching Assistants (NTA), which can be very much a misnomer given the excellent teaching which some are capable of carrying out. Currently the most common term is Learning Support Assistant (LSA). In some cases, the personnel involved may have had some formal training and years of practical experience working with various specialists. At the other extreme, they may have had no training at all and very little relevant experience of dealing with pupils with special educational needs. Some Support Assistants may have received initial training and a qualification for working with very young children and this is not always relevant when working across the curriculum at Key Stage 2. It would appear that, in many cases, the most skilled teaching is required from those who are receiving the least training and support. Given the range of duties and tasks which a Support Assistant may be required to carry out, you will need to ascertain what skills, knowledge and personal qualities need to be developed, so that they can confidently fulfil the demands of the role.

The example of a job description for a Support Assistant in Figure 10.2 gives an idea of the scope of such a post and also holds implications not only as to how you deploy such a person, but also the training that is necessary and for which you may be at least partly responsible.

Of course it is up to you, your headteacher and governors what you put into any job specification. It will, however, be up to

FIG 10.2
Specimen job description for a Support Assistant

The duties and responsibilities of support assistants will vary from school to school. The following is an example of what such a description might include

Specific Duties
1. Supervision of pupils in a variety of learning on social contexts.
2. Assisting staff to prepare and carry out programmes of work to meet pupils' needs.
3. Working with individual and small groups of pupils preparing, introducing supervising and monitoring tasks after consultation with teaching staff.
4. Supporting the development of pupil' skills and promoting positive attitudes towards learning.
5. Assisting pupils' integration into the group or class.
6. To provide feedback to enhance pupils' self-esteem.
7. Assisting in the monitoring of pupil's or group of pupils' performance and progress.
8. To encourage and to help develop appropriate behaviour.
9. To help pupils to develop positive relationships with other pupils and adults.
10. To assist and encourage pupils in their self-care, personal hygiene and independence.
11. To ensure pupil safety.
12. To help pupils to use classroom equipment safely.
13. To contribute to the maintenance of systematic accurate up-to-date records of pupils' progress and achievement.
14. To liaise with parents and to communicate clearly and sensitively with them.
15. To attend case conferences and reviews when necessary.

General Duties
1. To accompany pupils on educational visits and out of school activities.
2. To assist in the routine care of equipment and materials.
3. To help in preparing and clearing away teaching equipment and materials before and after teaching sessions.
4. To keep the work base tidy and the resources well organised.
5. To assist with or to undertake the attractive presentation and display of children's work.
6. To assist in the general supervision of pupils at breaks and lunchtimes.
7. To assist in the care of pupils awaiting collection by parents.
8. To attend staff meetings and inservice courses when requested by the headteacher or the LEA.

you to establish the roles and responsibilities of the Support Assistants with them (and your staff, governors and parents). This includes their relationships to pupils, parents, teachers and you as SENCO. You will have to determine the extent to which they will be involved in 'helping children learn' and in direct teaching. This latter has always been a controversial area, but there is now increasing acceptance that a Support Assistant can carry out certain teaching/instructional activities under the direction of a teacher. Certainly, in order to assist pupils, Support Assistants will need to:

- know and understand how to implement the school's SEN policy;
- understand key aspects of the National Curriculum;
- understand the National Literacy Strategy;
- learn about some major approaches to teaching literacy, oracy and mathematics;
- know something about the educational, social and emotional implications of the special educational needs of children in the school;
- appreciate and understand how to implement the school's Behaviour Policy/Code of Conduct;
- develop skills in observing pupils;
- develop skills of reporting to you and teachers about children's progress.

Fox (1996) reminds Support Assistants that their aim is not to do work for the pupils, but to enable them to do the tasks themselves. Based upon her advice we suggest the following strategies:

- Do as little as possible for the pupil, as learning comes from doing things for oneself including making mistakes.
- Clarify tasks if the pupil has not understood.
- Intervene only to avoid frustration.
- Make sure the pupil is on time, has the necessary equipment, or knows where it is kept and how to use it safely and correctly.
- Ensure that the task is one at which the pupil can succeed, but is not so easy that the pupil is not challenged.
- Link the learning to some aspect which is familiar and relevant.
- Help the pupil to organise thoughts and to consider how to structure and set out the work.
- Help the pupil to process the information by guided questioning and guided discovery.
- Give the pupil strategies to help them to remember.
- Be positive, praising freely for effort, success, perseverance, but not praising falsely or insincerely.

The main concerns of Support Assistants regarding their roles are:

■ a lack of clarity regarding their responsibilities and tasks when they are supporting in class;
■ not being sufficiently well informed or prepared when supporting pupils in class;
■ a lack of clarity regarding some of the school procedures, rules and routines;
■ not being regarded as a member of a team responsible for meeting the SEN of pupils whom they are supporting.

A very useful role for you as SENCO could be to help Support Teachers and Support Assistants clarify their roles. Challen and Majors (1997) recommend that help in exploring and clarifying their role could be part of the training for Support Assistants. Ask them:

a) to list the tasks and responsibilities which they are currently required to carry out;
b) to write down those aspects which are clear and those which are 'fuzzy'.

You could begin to plan what arrangements might be needed to:

■ help them become members and partners in the special needs team or department;
■ help them in working positively and constructively with parents;
■ help them contribute to the development of IEPs and reviews;
■ ensure that the school procedures are made known to them;
■ ensure that they are invited to relevant meetings;
■ ensure that opportunities are provided for training and professional development;
■ help colleagues to make effective use of the Support Assistants.

More specific training may be needed to help them to support particular pupils:

■ by involving the assistant in setting targets;
■ by helping them develop systems for monitoring and evaluating programmes;

- helping them to develop recording systems;
- helping them to develop reward systems.

Implementing your support strategy involves not only training learning support teachers and assistants, but also classroom teachers who have to learn to work cooperatively with another adult in their classroom. Using staff development time for joint exploration of the issues and methods introduced in this chapter is one way to do this. Where a class teacher may only have support for 30 minutes a week, it is important that this time is used effectively rather than dismissed as 'insignificant'.

Thomas (1985) draws attention to the considerable gains when additional personnel in the classroom follow 'room management (RM) procedures'. He identifies three roles during possible activity periods, those of Individual Helper, Activity Manager and Mover.

Individual Helper

The Individual Helper concentrates on working with an individual pupil for 5–15 minutes. This means that in 1 hour it should be possible to arrange between 4–12 individual teaching sessions.

- *Tasks (before the session)*:
    - has available a list of children for individual help and the activities and resources required;
    - helps the Activity Manager to organise the classroom;
    - assembles materials needed for each child's work in the area to be used for the individual work and sets out the activities ready for when each of the children arrive, e.g. four sets of activities for one group.
- *Tasks (during the sessions)*:
    - asks each of the children to come to the area to work (15 mins is thought to be the maximum for intensive work);
    - the emphasis is on positive teaching with plenty of praise and encouragement;
    - the next child is asked to come.

Activity Manager

The Activity Manager concentrates on the rest of the children, who will normally be organised in groups of between 4 and 8. She will quickly move around keeping them 'on task'.

- *Tasks (before the session)*:
  — organises a variety of tasks and activities for each group;
  — informs the others when she is ready to begin.
- *Tasks (during the session)*:
  — ensures that each group member has the appropriate resources to carry out tasks;
  — prompts individuals to start work;
  — supervises use of shared materials;
  — moves around the group to praise, reward those who are working appropriately;
  — gives minimum attention to those not engaged in the task.

Mover

The Mover may fetch more equipment, etc.; supervise emptying paint pots, sharpening pencils, etc.; deal with all interruptions, e.g. visitors, spillages, etc. This will leave the Individual Helper and the Activity Manager free from distraction. It may be that roles are changed within a session.

Monitoring and evaluating your support strategy

It is important to monitor the way in which in-class support is working. This can be done by meeting with groups and individuals and you should show how you make use of the evaluations of both support staff and classroom teachers. Regular meetings with support staff should also be held to:

- monitor and review pupil's progress; and
- provide a focus for further staff development.

in addition to ensuring that you are fully aware of how the strategy is working. You should report on how 'support' is operating in any report to the governors.

Chapter 11

Working in partnership with parents

In this chapter, as elsewhere in this book, the term parents is used for a child's immediate carers. It is acknowledged that these are not always a child's natural parents.

The Code of Practice emphasises the significance of the relationship between a school and the parents of children with special educational needs. Most primary schools have developed a range of ways of involving parents in school activities and their children's education, and your role as SENCO is certainly eased if you work in a school with strong and successful home–school relationships. Within the school's policy for parental involvement, a SENCO should ensure that particular arrangements exist for working closely 'as partners' with parents of children with SEN as recommended in the Code.

The concept of 'Partnership with Parents' was introduced in the Warnock Report (DES, 1978) and it is important for you to examine what this term means, if it is not to be a mere slogan. There is a wealth of literature on the topic of working with parents of children with SEN which provides not only useful frameworks for analysing your own understanding and practice, but also offers ideas for improving and extending practices. A short list of some recommended texts is given at the end of this chapter.

It is crucial to establish procedures for involving parents which recognise 'partnership' as a *two-way process* where both the school (represented by the SENCO and/or headteacher and/or class teacher) and parents are needed to make contributions to improve a child's learning. The Code of Practice calls for a school's arrangements to take account of 'parents' wishes, feelings and knowledge' at all stages, and emphasises the need for parents to believe that their views are considered and valued. Working with parents of children with SEN draws extensively on a SENCO's interpersonal skills, particularly in showing empathy and giving positive feedback. It is important that you enable parents to understand how you make use of their knowledge of their child in the assessment and teaching strategies you adopt. Similarly they need to understand not only how you and others are trying to help their child, but also what part they may play in this.

Studies of parents of children with SEN show that the majority want to be actively involved in helping the child but do not always understand how they might do this. There is a tendency, therefore, for them to seek an 'expert', often feeling there is some 'cure' if only they can find it. Sadly, some parents believe that there is some mystery surrounding 'special education'. One of your greatest tasks, therefore, is to 'demystify' both the nature and assessments of a child's difficulties and demonstrate what steps can be taken to help the child.

Earlier chapters of this book have drawn attention to ways in which parents should be formally involved in a school's SEN arrangements. The Code of Practice identifies three areas which a school should address:

- Information
- Partnership
- Access for Parents

We suggest that you might use the Code's suggestions as the basis for evaluating your school's practices.

Reviewing your school's arrangements for work with parents of children with SEN

Study the list below (based on para. 2.33 of the Code). Ask yourself the following questions for each statement:

(i) What does my school do about this?

(ii) How *well* does it do it?

Use your answers to draw up an Action Plan for improvements.

Information

- on the school's SEN policy
- on the support available for children with special educational needs within the school and LEA
- on parents' involvement in assessment and decision-making, emphasising the importance of their contribution
- on services such as those provided by the local authority for children 'in need'
- on local and national voluntary organisations which might provide information, advice and counselling

Partnership

- arrangements for recording and acting upon parental concerns
- procedures for involving parents when a concern is first expressed within the school
- arrangements for incorporating parents' views in assessment and subsequent reviews

Access for parents

- information in a range of community languages
- information on tape for parents who may have literacy or communication difficulties
- a parents' room or other arrangements in the school to help parents feel confident and comfortable

Of particular importance when working with parents is to find time to be able to listen to what they say. Good listening skills are essential for a SENCO and when parents know that they are being listened to, they are likely to feel valued and, in turn, perceive that you are a caring and concerned teacher. In other words, there is a reciprocal relationship whereby they listen to and value what you say. Parents of children with SEN often complain that teachers (and other professionals) do not

- listen
- understand
- communicate fully to them (give clear information)
- seem competent to meet a child's special educational needs.

All too often a major cause of these complaints are based on problems of communication. Sometimes this may lie in the fact that professionals do not present information in a clear and

One of the major aspects of the role of SENCO is to ensure that parents are not only listened to, but that they know they have the right to be listened to.

easily understood form. This is an area where you can ensure that you improve your own communication skills and improve all relevant documentation. However, another contributory factor to communication difficulties may be that a parent may be so emotionally involved in seeking help for their child that they cannot listen fully or comprehend the information they are given. They may be upset, feel incompetent, or be angry and frustrated. As a result they may bring 'emotional baggage' to a meeting which is not necessarily related to anything the school has or has not done, but this emotion 'blocks' or interferes with the communication process. It is important that all teachers are aware of this, and understand, therefore, that although they have approached a meeting with parents in a calm, helpful and supportive manner, ideas and suggestions may be met with misunderstanding and even rejection. An appreciation of the depth of concerns and anxieties of many parents may help clarify the nature of support which a SENCO can offer.

A SENCO should make sure that parents not only know about their child's school's SEN policy and practices, but how this fits into the LEA procedures. They need to know what LEA services are available to offer support to their child and how these relate to a staged process of assessment. Similarly they should be advised about the voluntary agencies which may offer support. An important resource for parents is the (free) booklet from the DfEE which might be one of the first documents you give them. (This booklet is available in several languages and there are also taped and Braille versions available.)

Although parents can obtain all the above information from their LEA and its Parent Partnership Scheme (to which a SENCO should also direct them), many parents respond better to such advice given by the SENCO who knows their child and has experience of their learning context rather than an LEA 'official'. Moreover, in offering them help, you are seen to be working 'with' parents, leading in turn to an increase of parents' confidence in your competence and assurance of support.

Because most primary SENCOs are also class teachers, it is often difficult to negotiate time to meet parents, even for statutory reviews. Several schools now attempt to release a SENCO for some period of time on a regular basis and you should endeavour to negotiate for this.

An earlier chapter dealt with the management of meetings and reviews. Sometimes, however, a meeting with a parent may be less formal, involving only you and a parent, or you and another professional and a parent. Such meetings often take place when a teacher is registering concern at Stage 1, or at the request of the parent who is concerned about a child not currently on the SEN Register, or where a parent is seeking information about progress before a formal review is due. It is worth developing a system for preparing for and recording such meetings. A meeting plan or schedule is not only useful for later reference, but also helps you to use the meeting time more efficiently. The following guidance and parent meeting record has been found useful by many primary school SENCOs.

Preparing for a meeting or 'conference' with a parent

1. Prepare a 'record-sheet' (as provided below) or agenda so that you can come to the meeting well prepared and can keep the meeting focused.
2. Record the purpose of the meeting (to clarify your own thinking and to help you keep the focus). Make sure that parents are aware of the purpose in advance and ask if they would like to include any other matters.
3. Find out about parents' availability *before* deciding upon the time and venue.
4. Prepare any papers and documentation you will use in advance and make sure parents have a copy. (Remember that for Annual Reviews it is a requirement that parents are furnished with any documentation others may have.) Have you taken the language of the home into account?
5. Advise the parents about who will be attending the meeting and *why*. Make sure they know whether the meeting is for 'advice/help' for the school or whether it is a formal meeting relating to a review.
6. Even when this is a meeting at a very early stage it may be 'good practice' to suggest they can bring a friend, relative or neighbour as it often helps to have someone to 'talk over' anything said at the meeting. However, try to make this suggestion in a way which does not imply the meeting will

discuss something which could be interpreted as 'bad news' or threatening.

7. Jot down some questions/topics you wish to ensure are covered during the meeting. As a main aim of any such meeting will be to *listen* to the parent, it is important to make sure that your concerns are also discussed. This pre-planning helps to focus the meeting.

8. Make a list of any of the pupil's work/books which you wish to refer to during the meeting (and then make sure you collect them prior to the start of the meeting). It is always useful to show parents examples of a child's work to illustrate strengths, difficulties and progress.

9. Make sure that you are fully aware of any procedures, nature of services and organisations which may be referred to during a meeting so that you feel competent in answering queries.

A written record of a meeting with parents is often useful, not only for you but for a parent who may:

■ seek reassurance that there has been mutual understanding of the outcomes of any meeting;

■ need to confirm what was actually said and achieved at a meeting this is particularly necessary where a parent is emotionally upset during the meeting and may, therefore, be unclear as to what was actually said);

■ be concerned to see that *action* will follow the meeting and the part(s) to be played in this by both parent and school.

During the meeting it is important to use your communication/interpersonal skills described earlier in this book to make sure that parents feel their opinions and feelings are valued and that you make every attempt to understand their viewpoints. It is particularly helpful, therefore, to use reflective listening and clarification skills. Above all it is important for parents to see that they have been instrumental in any decision making — all too often, parents believe they are merely invited to hear a decision already made by the professionals.

In an earlier chapter (p. 40), attention was drawn to the need to review your school's written communication to parents. In order to support parents within the SEN process, you might consider preparing a booklet or guidance sheet for parents

Record of Meeting with Parent/Carer

Pupil's name.. Date of Birth..

Home language..

Date of Meeting..

Place..

Present..

....

Purpose of Meeting

Questions/Topics for discussion

Pupil's work/books to bring to the meeting

Questions asked by/information from parents

Agreed action to be taken:

By SENCO:

By Parents:

Date of next meeting..

Signed:..SENCO

....Parent/Carer

© Falmer Press

when, for example, they attend a review meeting. Very often a parent may be bemused on looking at an IEP with its targets and review dates, and find themselves uncertain as to what questions to ask the SENCO at review. Rather than put yourself into a position where you (and perhaps others) *tell* parents about IEP, such guidance might empower parents. The following set of questions might form the basis of a guidance sheet. You may construct similar advice or questions for parents to ask in relation to other procedures.

A Parent's Guide to IEPs for Planning and Review

An IEP is an Individual Education Plan for your child. You might like to ask these questions when looking at the IEP for your child. If you are uncertain about or unhappy with any part of the IEP please ask me or your class teacher to explain more fully.

1. What arrangements are made to help the child?
2. How is progress monitored? Who is responsible for monitoring progress?
3. How much have I contributed to drawing up the plan?
4. Have my views been taken into account?
5. How much account has been taken of my child's views and ideas?
6. How much progress is my child making? Is it enough?
7. Is a review date shown? How many 'reviews' can there be before moving up a stage?
8. Are these targets relevant to my child's needs?

SENCO's name
Coordinator for SEN

Parents of children with SEN benefit greatly when their children are in schools which hold regular meetings with parents, including parents' evenings and workshops. Parents of children new to a school, may, for example, be invited to a meeting where the head and staff outline several of the school's policies. Many primary schools offer open days or evenings where the curriculum is explained and these occasions provide an opportunity for the SENCO to explain 'differentiation' and demonstrate some of the methods and materials that are used to support access to the curriculum. This is an excellent opportunity for all parents to learn about the school's SEN provision.

Where a school has introduced projects such as 'Paired Reading', involving parents and/or grandparents, there are advantages for the parents of children with SEN because their children are included in a school-wide scheme rather than being 'treated differently'. Reading workshops have often been useful not only in raising children's achievement, but also in improving family attitudes to literacy (and in some cases raising literacy levels of parents). Where parents can be 'taught' the skills of teaching reading, writing and maths, then they feel more confident in their own role in supporting their child. Very often parents of children with SEN want to help their child but do not know *how* to do so. This is particularly true also for parents of children with emotional and behaviour difficulties. Very often (although not always) these behaviours are exhibited in the home and parents do not know how to manage them. As a result they are often dealt with inconsistently, sometimes met by aggression and physical punishment, sometimes ignored. Such behaviours often leave parents feeling under stress and incompetent. When faced by teachers also telling them how difficult it is to manage their children's behaviour, they react either by withdrawing from the situation (not attending meetings, telling the teacher that it's up to the professionals, 'blaming the school') or by being aggressive — again often 'blaming the school'.

The number of exclusions from primary schools for reasons of behaviour difficulties has risen in recent years. The Green Paper *Excellence for All* (DfEE, 1997) devotes a whole chapter to the area of emotional and behaviour difficulties and acknowledges that many of the causes may lie in family and social factors. Nevertheless, the Elton Report (DES, 1989) emphasised that schools can make a considerable difference to both the incidence (and prevention) of problem behaviours and to managing behaviour. All schools now have a Behaviour or Discipline Policy.

Many children referred to the SENCO may have been identified as presenting behaviour difficulties. One of the SENCO's responsibilities, therefore, will be to make assessments of these and, where necessary, help a class teacher to draw up an appropriate Individual Education Plan or Individual Behaviour Plan to improve a pupil's conduct. Parents will, of course, be consulted and may well throw useful light on the behaviours. This is particularly so where perhaps some family circumstances has triggered a behaviour problem. Some schools involve parents in a programme to manage the pupil's behaviour in both home and school, as part of an IEP. A few have adopted an approach, more commonly found in special schools, of establishing a 'parents' support group' where parents can share concerns and management strategies with others and, through workshops, led by the SENCO or the school's educational psychologist, learn how to manage children's behaviour and build their self-esteem appropriately.

It is worth considering a variety of ways in which the school's general arrangements for parental involvement can include approaches that may hold particular significance for children with SEN, as utilising these arrangements:

- makes less demand on a SENCO's time;
- reduces the concerns of some parents that *they* are 'different' and their child's needs can only be met by 'very special and different' methods;
- reassures parents that their children are in an 'inclusive' school.

Of course it is also true that a SENCO will encounter some parents who appear aggressive, who may be only too aware of their rights and who may appear to have a lot of knowledge about their child's difficulties. It is very easy, particularly for a new SENCO, to feel threatened by this. If your initial approach as a caring, sympathetic listener and helper meets little success, then you may need to draw on other interpersonal skills for dealing with conflict. You may need to be more assertive.

It is important to recognise that you may sometimes be faced with real dilemmas and feel trapped between school, parents and the LEA. This is particularly likely when parents are seeking resources which are not readily available, but which you perhaps feel *would* be useful in meeting a child's needs. Helping parents to know and seek their rights may not be perceived as 'helpful' by your school or LEA! In such circumstances you must attempt to be accurate, objective and professional in providing any evidence you have about the pupil's needs and progress.

You will find that the DfEE *Handbook for SENCOs* (DfEE, 1997a) offers useful guidance on working with parents.

Throughout, a SENCO's responsibility is to coordinate provision to identify and meet a child's needs. Every attempt must be made, therefore, to establish and maintain good working relationships with parents. Where a stressful situation does arise, you may need to call upon the headteacher or a member of the external support agencies for help in resolving interpersonal difficulties. Fortunately such situations should be rare, and your expectations of work with parents should be based on an assumption that teachers and parents share a common concern — that of helping a child to achieve success.

This chapter has emphasised the management of arrangements for involving parents and proposed a need for formal and visible procedures. However, the key to working with parents is the development of good interpersonal relationships based on trust and an acknowledgment of the contributions both teachers and parents can make to a child's learning. It is important to acknowledge the way in which informal meetings and 'chats' (even of very short duration) can foster good working relationships. Greeting parents when they bring children to (or collect them from) school, where interest is shown in family activities, and brief comments made about activities and progress, takes very little time but can establish an easy rapport which breaks through potential barriers in more formal situations. Informal encounters and 'incidental' comments in playgrounds and corridors have been found invaluable by primary SENCOs.

Recommended reading on working with parents

BLAMIRES, M., ROBERTSON, C. and BLAMIRES, J. (1997) *Parent–Teacher Partnership: Practical Approaches to Meet Special Educational Needs*, London: David Fulton.

GASCOIGNE, E. (1995) *Working with Parents as Partners in SEN*, London: David Fulton.

HORNBY, G. (1995) *Working with Parents of Children with Special Needs*, London: Cassell.

WOLFENDALE, S. (Ed.) (1997) *Working with Parents of SEN Children after the Code of Practice*, London: David Fulton.

Chapter 12	Working with other professionals and outside agencies

Introduction

A crucial aspect of the management and coordination role of a SENCO is your involvement with a range of other professionals and external support services and agencies. No other subject leader in a primary school will be expected to

- have a working knowledge of
- work cooperatively with
- manage and coordinate
- initiate and establish relationships with
- advise parents about

so many different professionals and agencies, including voluntary organisations. A school's SEN policy should make explicit the way in which the school relates to such services and, in the case of relevant health and education services, should specify the nature of support available at particular Stages of SEN Assessment and Provision.

It is essential, therefore, for a SENCO to become familiar with the immediate local services and know the name of the first 'point of contact'. Efforts should be made to meet appropriate named personnel 'face-to-face' in order to:

- establish a relationship;
- explore the extent and limits of the role;
- find out how the service (and individuals within it) operate.

Such first-hand experience proves more useful than the information gleaned from an agency's publications, although reading any booklets or leaflets available from these services would clearly be useful preparation to any meeting, so that you are aware of the aims and general services available before you enter any meeting. Such preparation will also help you plan your questions in advance. There are certain key questions to which you need answers if you are to work effectively (and efficiently) with other professionals, and these will also help you to advise parents and your colleagues.

Questions to ask external services and agencies:

- *What* services can you provide for
  — the school in general?
  — specific pupils?
  — their families?
  What is the nature and form of the services?
- Under what circumstances are these provided? For example:
  — is the support available for *all* children or only those with SEN?
  — is this 'routine' free provision?
  — is there a cost?
  — is the support for:
    - children?
    - parents?
    - teachers?
  — is there an implication that a child must be at a particular Stage of the school's (or LEA's) SEN policy before this support is available?
- Who is the contact person? (and what is their telephone number?)
- What procedures should be followed in making a referral or request for support?
- What information would the service require from the school and in what form? (e.g. a written assessment report or a brief, oral description), i.e. How can we help *you* to work more effectively with children and their families?

You might like to add further questions.

Mention has already been made of the need to include voluntary organisations among the list of services available, particularly where there may be local associations or groups, as these often provide important support networks for parents.

Not all statutory services will be provided by the LEA, and it is important to discover the schools contact systems with the health services and social services. This information is readily available from your local education office.

It is, nevertheless, likely that the most common and important form of support will come from SEN support services provided by the LEA. These services:

> *can play an important part in helping schools identify, assess and make provision for children with special educational needs. Such services include specialist teachers of children with hearing, visual and speech and language impairments, teachers in more general learning and behaviour support services, educational psychologists and advisers or teachers with a knowledge of information technology for children with special educational needs.* (DFE, 1994a, 2.58, p. 20)

Not all LEAs can offer the breadth of services suggested above, although educational psychology services are mandatory. As SENCO, you must be aware of what provision is available from such services and also whether there are alternative forms of specialist support. In some LEAs, for example, schools have formed 'clusters' to share expertise across a number of primary schools in one geographical area; in others, there may be 'clusters' of special and mainstream schools where there may be:

- arrangements to facilitate 'integration' of pupils from special schools into mainstream on a full or part-time basis;
- opportunities for a range of specialist support from consultancy and advice, to visits to schools and sharing of practices and materials, to provision of support teaching as part of 'outreach' work from a specialist school.

Another valuable source of advice and support for a SENCO and school staff (rather than direct intervention with children and parents) is the LEA Advisory Service. The SEN Adviser can offer support for the SENCO role within a school and offer practical advice about methods of assessment, teaching and LEA resources. They also often provide, or are aware of, local opportunities for continuing professional development for SENCOs *and* other staff.

In Chapter 7 we recommended that a SENCO should keep a file or record of the names and addresses (and contact names and telephone numbers) of all available support. Chapter 14 provides a list of national voluntary agencies which will be of particular use to parents, as well as giving teachers information about a range of disabilities. It is particularly important for you to keep a record of the services and agencies which you and your school can draw on for help. You might use a format such as that below:

Service and address. Contact name: Tel. No.	Support available for:	Nature of support:

Local services and agencies

The following are the local services and agencies most commonly found, but you should draw up a list appropriate to your school. The SEN Adviser/SEN Officer of the LEA will be able to provide much of this as a starting point. Some will change/be added as you make further contacts and, of course, as personnel and even services change. A SENCO needs to be not only aware of these services but understand the distinctive contribution each brings to meeting a child's special educational needs.

List of Local Services and Agencies

Education
SEN Adviser   —
SEN Named Officer   —
SEN Statementing Officer   —
Parent Partnership Coordinator/Officer   —
Educational Psychologist(s)   —
Education Welfare Officer   —
Learning Support Service(s)
- Learning Support (general) (or Moderate Learning Difficulties)
- Sensory Impaired Service (may be separate for Hearing and Visual Impairment)
- Specific Learning Difficulties
- Speech and Language Difficulties
- Behaviour Support Services
Schools/Units
- Outreach/special school services
- Pupil Referral Units

Home Tuition Service
Hospital School Service
Section 11/Multilingual Services
Travellers' Services
Portage Services (for young children)

Social Services
Social Services Department
Child Protection Service
Disability Services
Additional Support Teams (e.g. for behavioural management)
Nursery/Early Education Centres

Health Services
Schools Medical Officer
Speech and Language Therapists
School nurse/doctor
Community Paediatrician
Occupational Therapist
Physiotherapist
Child/Family Centres (Psychiatric Services)
Health Visitors (particularly for pre-school)

Multi-professional Centres/Services
Particularly for preschool children, e.g. Child Development or Assessment Centres

It is probably at Stage 3 and beyond that a SENCO will work most closely with external services and particular individuals and it is almost certain that the number of professionals working with any one child and family will be much smaller than the above list implies. However, it is worth noting that although you may be working collaboratively with only a small number of professionals, parents may be involved with many more. So, if you can find ways of reducing the amount of information requested from parents, this may reduce stress and reassure them that there really is a 'multi-professional or inter-disciplinary team' providing coherent support.

Not all professionals share the same philosophy or even focus on special educational needs, and it is helpful to try to understand the perspectives and models underpinning different ways of working. Like teachers in schools, other professionals may be experiencing the frustrations of heavy workloads, increasing demands and diminishing resources. Trying to get to know individuals within the services can often improve mutual respect and break down some of the professional barriers which may otherwise arise as a result of differences in

■ priorities and philosophies;
■ functions served by agencies/schools;
■ ways (and hows) of working.

Multi-disciplinary assessment

It is at Stage 4 of the Code of Practice (a request for statutory assessment) that there is evidence of the involvement of several agencies representing several disciplines. Nevertheless, even at this stage, assessments are nearly always carried out independently by different professionals. Davie (1993) has summarised some of the different ways in which health and social services have approached assessment, event in the field of special educational needs. However, there is a statutory duty for collaboration under both the Education Act of 1993 and the 1989 Children Act. Whilst it is still disappointing that the 1989 Children Act described children 'in need' somewhat differently from the earlier definition of special educational needs given in the 1981 Education Act, there are several aspects which point to common concerns and the benefits of interdisciplinary assessment.

Nevertheless, reports at Stage 4 all too often reflect independent assessments, and medical reports in particular are often written without reference to educational implications. At best the arrangements appear to be within loose networks. An exception may often be found in pre-school assessments where there may be more evidence of teamwork, particularly from Child Development Centres. In primary schools, however, it is often at the *intervention* stages (Stages 3 and 5), and then largely through the coordination and management skills of a SENCO, that there is greater evidence of multi-professional or interdisciplinary cooperation. Where possible, as SENCO, you should attempt to hold case conferences and reviews where professionals from all the services working with the child can meet with the parent(s) and comment on progress and contribute towards setting the next target. Whilst it is recognised that there are some difficulties in arranging for busy professionals to meet on an agreed date, experience shows a large degree of satisfaction from all concerned — particularly parents — where this does occur.

Securing effective working relationships

We suggest that the notion of securing effective working relationships with multi-professional agencies must be based on strong working partnerships with parents and therefore will be planned with parents.

Six steps to working with external support agencies:

1. *Find out as much as possible about which services are available and what they offer.*
   - LEA information available
   - National voluntary organisations
   - Parent–Partnership schemes
   - documentation from all the above
   - meetings and discussions with professionals from all these services and agencies.

2. *Introduce yourself to them and outline your role and school's policy.* Provide them with a copy of the policy and describe the

school's practices within the context. Let them know what the 'school's resources' are for SEN (time, physical/material and human).

Other agencies need to be aware of the curriculum and the nature and range of support offered
- within the school, and
- by support services already working with a pupil.

3. *Consider and discuss ways in which you could work together.* You need to be aware of the expectations of both the parents *and* your teacher colleagues when drawing up suggestions.

4. *The Code of Practice mentions drawing up 'service level agreements'* (a form of contract) to formalise arrangements and some formally agreed statement is useful. This sort of agreement specifies
- the *nature* of support available
- for whom (names of pupils and stages of the SEN Register, monitoring of staff, etc.)
- time available to the school (days/times)

You should also be aware of the service's expectations of you/the school
- availability of staff and/or pupils — if there is a school visit involving particular children/staff on a particular day and they happen to be absent, you should inform the external service so that their time is not wasted on a visit. Similarly you need to be informed if the external professional is ill or unavoidably prevented from coming to your school.

The objectives of the service should be stated clearly so that it is possible for you and the service provider to evaluate and review the service.

5. *Parents must be involved at all stages and kept fully informed* (including involvement in the review and evaluation exercise).

6. *Plan for continuity and ensure that there is due consideration of all transition points.* There are, for example, some services which operate only at preschool or secondary school levels whereas you deal mainly with primary school support. You need to be aware of (as do parents) any differences in the nature of provision. (In some LEAs, a child may receive the support from an external support service in Year 6 (because needs cannot be met by the primary school's own resources), yet in Year 7 of a secondary school such support may not be available. However, the secondary school may have sufficient resources, (e.g. a SENCO with available time, additional Learning Support Teachers) to meet the child's needs, or a child may make

Suggestion

Preparing to work with other professionals

Develop a set of statements and questions as the basis for developing stronger working relationships with other professionals.

In particular, find out:

- what information they will require from a school;
- what form this information should take;
- the nature of the services (and time) they offer to the school.

sufficient progress to be placed at a lower stage on an SEN Register. It is important that a parent is fully aware of the circumstances surrounding any decisions affecting the nature and source of provision. Where they do not, or they see no marked improvement in their child's attainment, they are highly likely to be concerned at what they perceive as a reduction in provision or neglect (or ignorance) of their child's needs. Much, therefore, relies on your ability to keep parents fully involved in decision making and aware of the context.

This aspect of a SENCO's role offers a challenge and it is difficult to describe here the nature of external support from multi-professional services because there are considerable local variations. Some SENCOs may find that only the headteacher deals with external agencies and you need to ensure that the principles underpinning such contacts are consistent with your philosophy and policy about SEN. Good relationships with external agencies are essential, not only to meeting children's SEN, but to effective partnerships with parents and to maintaining SEN provision of a high quality.

Chapter 13

Supporting and maintaining quality

Developing and maintaining provision of high quality for meeting children's special education needs does not depend solely on your ability to implement appropriate procedures. We have emphasised throughout this book that your responsibilities for coordinating SEN provision do not hold total responsibility for meeting pupils' needs. The Code of Practice makes it clear that all staff share this responsibility. The Green Paper *Excellence for All Children* (DfEE, 1997a) reiterates this:

> *. . . a SENCO cannot do everything single-handedly. It is the responsibility of all teachers and support staff in a school*
> - *to be aware of the school's responsibilities for children with special educational needs;*
> - *to have regard to the guidance in the Code of Practice;*
> - *to apply that guidance effectively in assessing and teaching children with SEN; and*
> - *to work together in the classroom to raise standards for all pupils.*
> (DfEE, 1997a, p. 61)

Earlier in this book, particularly in the sections on support teaching (see pp. 162–70) we have pointed to ways in which you can give direction to staff in meeting their responsibilities, and, by working jointly, using a 'problem-solving' approach, increase their confidence in their own teaching abilities to meet the individual learning needs of children. You can encourage them to secure successful relationships with children by demonstration and share teaching strategies and techniques through joint planning and Individual Educational Plans.

In this chapter, we suggest that you consider the part of your role that carries some responsibility for the professional development of staff, as this is integral to developing and maintaining special educational provision of high quality. Meeting SEN in mainstream schools is heavily dependent on confident, competent staff.

Who needs professional development?

A useful starting point is to consider who needs professional development in SEN, in order to establish the nature of their needs. Consider the needs of the following:

■ governors
■ all classroom teachers
■ teachers (including part-time) who may have some lessons each week designated for 'learning support' or specialist SEN teaching (in-class or withdrawal)
■ learning support assistants
■ supply teachers
■ experienced teachers who come 'new' to your school
■ newly qualified teachers (NQTs)
■ yourself as SENCO (to meet the TTA's standards and continue to develop as a reflective practitioner).

Certainly all your teaching colleagues will be more effective and your workload will be reduced if they
■ can identify and assess individual needs;
■ can meet diverse needs through their teaching, e.g. curriculum differentiation;
■ have knowledge and understanding of the SEN of particular children and the effects on their learning;
■ can contribute to the production of an IEP;
■ know how to implement, monitor and review IEPs;
■ report effectively to and work effectively with parents;
■ raise children's self-esteem through their teaching and all interactions;
■ know how to manage non-teachers and LSAs in their classrooms.

You might add to this list and also consider what constituent areas of knowledge and skills underlie the above.

Earlier we cautioned you not to feel that SENCOs should have to be 'all-knowing' and should not cast yourself in the role of expert as this might mean that staff do not assume their responsibilities for meeting pupils' special educational needs. Involvement in planning for colleagues' professional development in SEN can give rise to staff concerns where they may question where their responsibilities end and yours begin. We suggested in the first chapter that such tensions can be reduced when your role is made explicit and where there are clear procedures related to school policy. Nevertheless, many teachers, including some very experienced staff may still feel anxious and professionally challenged when they encounter some children's difficulties, and you need to demonstrate where and how you are able to offer to support them. They also need to see that the professional development offered in SEN is there to help them carry out their teaching more effectively, and will not result in any diminution of your support for them.

Who plans and delivers the professional development?

You may find that you are not only asked to advise the headteacher (or professional development coordinator) as to appropriate continuing professional development for staff, but to organise and/or deliver inservice training. It is quite common for a SENCO to organise both short 'twilight' sessions and whole-day programmes as part of the school's professional development plan. The issue as to whether you deliver the inservice activity yourself or invite an outside specialist will depend largely on:

■ the purpose of the in-service, and
■ the topic.

Where you feel sufficiently competent and confident in your knowledge and experience to offer training personally, there is an advantage in that you know the audience (teachers, governors, non-teaching assistants, learning support assistants) and the school's policies and procedures. You can therefore adopt the materials and delivery styles which you know will be appropriate. Direct personal intervention in delivery is particularly effective when you are discussing improving school practices and sharing teaching methodologies. Part of such an activity can be the production of a teaching plan or action plan to ensure there will be an impact on the school. However, if, for example, you have recently discovered that a child is dyspraxic, and wish to inform all staff about this area, you may wish to call upon an external specialist, or a teacher from another school who has considerable experience of working with children with dyspraxia. Another occasion on which it may be useful to invite an external speaker might be where you know that the topic is controversial and introduces ideas which you know may be unpopular with some staff. Using an outside consultant means that all staff (including you) can engage in debating issues rather than identifying a member of staff with those issues. In distinguishing ideas from staff personalities there will be greater opportunity for open discussion without disturbing staff relationships.

Identifying professional development needs

Professional development is now seen as integral to a school's development plan and the drive towards school improvement. Raising pupils' achievements, particularly in literacy and numeracy, is a national priority and inevitably there is a role in this for SENCOs. Planning continuing professional development (CPD) activities (formerly described as inservice education of teachers or INSET) should be undertaken in cooperation with your school's professional development coordinator.

Sometimes there can be tensions between a school's perceptions of professional development needs to serve the school's priorities and staff's perceptions of their own personal professional needs. However, teachers, on the whole, accept that where school or directed time is to be used for professional development, then the activities will be related to the school's needs. It is important, however, to try to ensure that any decisions to be made about the purpose and topic of any planned CPD activity are clear and involve staff. It is one

This questionnaire has been designed to help identify staff's needs for professional development to enable us to meet the special educational needs of our pupils more effectively. Please complete the form and return it to me by _____ .
Results of this survey will form the basis of our meeting on _____ . Thank you.

Area/topic	I am confident about	I am concerned about	I would like to know more about	I would like further training on	I have taken further training on	I would not be interested in INSET in
Specific types of SEN e.g. learning difficulties						
Dyslexia						
Emotional/behaviour difficulties etc.						
Others (please specify)						
Curriculum differentiation						
Identification of learning difficulties						
Assessment of literacy difficulties						
Assessment of mathematics difficulties						
Teaching spelling to children with difficulties						
Managing pupils' behaviour						
Building self-esteem of pupils with learning difficulties						
Other (please specify)						

© The Manchester Metropolitan University, Didsbury School of Education

From: *Special Educational Needs: Putting the Code to Work*

FIG 13.1
SEN professional development questionnaire

thing for you to be convinced of the need for professional development in a particular area — but this need should be shared, identified or at least understood by all those who will take part.

As a SENCO you can identify CPD needs in some of the following ways:

- direct questions / discussions with staff
- questionnaire (perhaps based on the information from Figure 13.1)
- analysing the nature of requests from staff over a period of time
- reviewing the SEN policy and practices and identifying weaknesses
- proposing areas identified in a variety of sources
- selecting topics / teaching methods which are 'new' and relatively unfamiliar to colleagues, e.g. ideas from recent professional journals for SEN
- recent reports, circulars etc.

The SEN Professional Development Questionnaire (Figure 13.1) (from Phillips and Cockett, 1995) may be useful as a model to discover staff's expressed needs where it is easy to demonstrate staff participation in directing professional development. Results can be fed back to them and priorities agreed.

In drawing up your proposal for the professional development programme, you should show consideration for colleagues by acknowledging their expertise and experience and also the diverse demands currently made upon them.

Planning professional development for a school — Preliminary questions

1. What is the identified need?
2. Who is the target audience?
3. How does the identified area (purpose and topic) relate to the prior experiences and knowledge of those involved?
4. What sort of activity could meet this need?
5. What form will the activity take?
6. How long and over what period of time will the activity take place?
7. How does this relate to the school's SEN policy, CPD plan / school development plan?

8. How will this programme be evaluated?
9. What other activities are planned to take place over the same period? (e.g. CPD for implementing the National Literacy Strategy)
10. Do I need to consult further before drawing up a proposal?

Planning your professional development programme

You may be required to produce a written proposal for your headteacher or governors, particularly where there may be financial implications. This needs to show that you have thought out not only the purpose of the programme but also the form it will take and the implications for organisation. If you are relatively inexperienced in delivering inservice, then you may find it useful to look at some of the published packages that are available. We have been involved in producing a set of materials (including video) specifically for SENCOs to use with staff in primary schools. This package, *Special Educational Needs: Putting the Code to Work* (Phillips and Cockett, 1995) contains full instructions for the person who will be delivering the activities and copies of materials for workshops including those for making handouts and overhead transparencies. Other packages we recommend include, *Building a Better Behaved School* (Galvin, Mercer and Costa, 1991) and a variety of materials from Framework Press.

A proposal for a professional development programme should include:

- the aim/intended outcome
- topic/area
- rationale (evidence to support this need)
- audience/participants
- provider/staffing (who will deliver / facilitate)
- content area/methods of delivery
- resources required
- time
- venue
- evaluation criteria
- costings (including fees (if involved) photocopying, refreshments.

Delivery styles/methods for professional development		
When are the following methods	most useful?	least useful?

1. Lecture/questions
2. Informal lecture/talk (i.e. with interruptions invited)
3. Problems/questions posed to discussion groups
4. Role play/simulations
5. Practical workshops
6. Demonstrations
7. Small group discussions
8. Brainstorming

Your proposal will, of course, need to consider the content and methods of delivery carefully to make sure they meet your aims and your audience's needs. You might find it useful to undertake the following activity to further your thinking about selecting appropriate content, methods and materials (enlarge the questionnaire to allow space for your answers). Add any other methods you can think of.

If you are not delivering the programme yourself, then many of the items listed in your general proposal will be addressed by the provider in discussion *with* you. It is important, however, that you can specify clearly

- the target audience (their current experiences and expertise in the area);
- the intended outcome (and how success is to be evaluated);
- the preferred styles of delivery.

You can then ask the provider for their proposal. You should keep a record of what has been agreed.

Evaluation

It is important to be able to evaluate the success or effectiveness of any professional development activity. There are several important dimensions to this:

1. Differentiating between evaluation of the activity itself and its impact (very often we find we evaluate the *day* or *course* rather than any effect on professional development or the school).

Evaluation of a Professional Development Activity

Title of course / activity

The stated purpose / aim / intended outcome of the activity

....

....

....

Date(s) ....

Venue

....

Personal evaluation of the activity (in relation to its stated aim / purpose)

Knowledge, skills, attributes gained

How will I use this / these in my role / classroom / school? (as applicable)

What impact do I expect this to make on (or for) pupils?

Do I wish to share anything from this activity with others? (i.e. to disseminate knowledge / skills / attributes to others)
Who?   When?   Why?

Follow-up evaluation after......months (3,6,12 — determine according to the intended outcome)

Date..   Signature ....

© Falmer Press

2. Is the intended outcome related to
    - attitudes?
    - practices?
    - pupil achievement / behaviour / attendance?
3. Short-term or long-term effects?
4. Impact on
    - teachers
    - children
    - others.

These points must be considered at the planning / proposal writing stage, and decisions taken about the criteria to be used in evaluation success. You might find it useful to draw up an evaluation sheet, such as the one below, which we suggest you complete by referring to a professional development activity or course you have taken recently.

Forms of professional development activities

It is interesting to note that when teachers are asked 'What constitutes professional development?' they often refer mainly to their school's five professional development days (formerly called 'Training Days'), twilight school-based INSET sessions, and courses run by their LEA or universities and colleges. You may, however, encourage them to think more widely, for example:

1. Reading of important newspapers and professional journals and books.
2. Informal and formal discussions with colleagues
    - in school;
    - at meetings across schools in clusters;
    - at conferences;
    - at meetings of professional associations.
3. Sharing ideas and experiences in joint-planning and co-teaching lessons.
4. Working collaboratively to develop resources.

Very often, the cooperation between a class teacher and SENCO leads to *mutual professional development*, and because it is often focused on meeting the needs of identified pupils, it is likely to make an impact on the child's learning. Despite a lack of research evidence that this experience is transmuted into knoweldge and skills that are transferred to general professional practice, there is widespread belief among teachers that this is so. Such professional development might be described as 'on-the-job training', and its significance should not be overlooked not only as part of the SEN policy but within the school's CPD policy.

A school which invests in planned professional development is likely to improve its effectiveness. It should be involved actively in self-assessment, and part of your role as SENCO is, of course, to monitor and review the quality of SEN provision in relation to meeting children's SEN. The TTA's National Standards for SENCOs (TTA, 1998) offers guidelines for the 'effective coordination of SEN' and you might find these useful in evaluating quality within your school.

External evaluation also takes place, of course, particularly from parents and LEA. In particular, there is external inspection from OFSTED, where part of the inspection process will examine SEN provision. A primary inspection team will rarely include a specialist in SEN unless a school has a 'unit' or 'resourced provision' for children with SEN. However, you should anticipate that the inspectors will be concerned with:

- the relationship between practices and the SEN policy;
- staff awareness of the school's procedures for identifying, assessing and meeting children's SEN;
- the extent to which SEN underpins and permeates the school's organisational structures and curriculum;
- working relationships between the staff and the SENCO;
- resources management in relation to the SEN policy and practice;
- curriculum differentiation;
- evidence of monitoring in relation to IEPs;
- procedures for assessment, recording and reporting for *all* pupils, to ensure that they meets the requirements for those children with SEN;
- liaison with external agencies and services;
- good relationships with parents (they will wish to know whether parents know who the SENCO is and who the 'responsible person' is (head or governor) for the school;
- whether staff have undertaken professional development in the area of SEN in the last two years.

OFSTED Inspection

Pre-inspection

The Registered Inspector who will lead the inspection will ask you for certain paperwork prior to inspection. This will include factual, financial and administrative details, including information about pupils' attainments in the National Curriculum, and information about pupils with SEN. The inspectors also hold a meeting with parents where they can find out about relationships and levels of satisfaction with the school.

Preparing for inspection: The SENCO's role

The inspectors may wish to meet you, or may ask for certain information. We suggest that you make sure you have the following *available* although you may not be asked for them:

- the SEN policy;
- the SEN register and computerised record(s), if used;
- a copy of the school's prospectus with paragraphs on SEN;
- copies of relevant paperwork to support the in-school procedures, including an overview of the systems which operate;
- SENCO job description and the job descriptions of any other staff, including part-time and support assistants who may have a role in SEN support (n.b. Circular 11/90 offers guidance on levels of staffing for SEN pupils with statements);
- information about the SEN budget and how it is allocated;
- examples of IEPs, records and samples of pupils' work;
- timetables of 'support' sessions;
- minutes of relevant meetings, e.g. reviews;
- information about links with other schools;
- information about links with external support services;
- details of any staff development in SEN over the last two years for you (and information about your qualifications) and the whole staff.

During the inspection

Inspectors may wish to see you and / or to examine any of the above documents. They are likely to:

- ask to see a sample of statements and IEPs and may wish to see the children and samples of work. They will be looking to see if the curriculum on offer meets the specific targets stated in the IEP;
- be looking, in all classrooms, for evidence that the curriculum meets the needs of *all* pupils;
- consider whether children with SEN have equal access to a balanced, differentiated and challenging curriculum;
- to investigate the use made of any specialist equipment and resources and whether accommodation, furnishing, acoustics etc., are appropriate for the children in the school.

If your policy is operating effectively, then an inspection should not mean 'extra work'. Rather, see it as an opportunity for your school to celebrate its success!

Professional development for a SENCO

As a professional, you are responsible for directing your own professional development. Whilst much of this comes from engagement in the processes and activities described in this book, you need to determine your *own* development needs. We hope this book will have helped your professional development in many ways, and that is has also served to help you decide where you require further training. This may be in any of the following areas:
- management
- interpersonal or counselling skills
- teaching methodologies
- delivering in-service training to others.

The newly published *National Standards for SENCOs* sets out clear expectations, and one of the aims of all national standards is to help teachers:

❝ ... *to plan and monitor their development, training and performance effectively, and to set clear, relevant targets for improving their effectiveness.* (TTA, 1998, p. 1)

The Standards provide a framework for your analysis of your own needs, perhaps in discussion with your headteacher or other colleagues. In the same way the Standards also:

> **❝** . . . *help providers of professional development to plan and provide high quality, relevant training.*   (TTA, 1998, p. 1)

You are therefore likely to find a range of appropriate training available from LEA, professional associations and institutes of higher education. Improving the quality of teaching and improving standards of achievement for *all* pupils is central to the role of the SENCO. It is crucial, therefore, that you recognise the need for your own professional development to continue.

We hope that this book has stimulated your thinking about your practice and has contributed towards both your own professional development and towards the improvement of SEN provision in your school. Not all the ideas will have been directly relevant to your school and your situation, but we hope there has been sufficient to encourage you towards further development for you, your colleagues and your pupils.

Part four   Resources

Chapter 14
List of voluntary associations
offering information and advice
for teachers and parents

Chapter 15
A SENCO's guide to using
the Internet

List of voluntary associations offering information and advice for teachers and parents

General advice

Advisory Centre for Education (ACE) Limited
Unit 1B
Aberdeen Studios
22 Highbury Grove
London N5 2EA
Tel: 0171 354 8321

CSIE Centre for Studies on Integration in Education
1 Redland Close
Elm Lane
Redland
Bristol BS6 6UE
Tel: 0117 923 8450

Contact a Family
170 Tottenham Court Road
London W1P OHA
Tel: 0171 383 3555

Council for Disabled Children
c/o National Children's Bureau
8 Wakley Street
London EC1V 7QU
Tel: 0171 278 9441

Disability Equality in Education
78 Mildmay Grove
London N1 4PJ

Disabled Living Foundation
380–384 Harrow Road
London W9 2HU
Tel: 0171 289 6111

Independent Panel for Special Education Advice (IPSEA)
22 Warren Hill Road
Woodbridge
Suffolk IP12 4DU

Integration Alliance — In Touch
10 Norman Road
Sale
Cheshire M33 3DF
Tel: 0161 962 4441

National Children's Bureau
8 Wakeley Street
London EC1V 7QE
Tel: 0171 278 9441

National Toy Libraries Association
66 Churchway
London NEW1 1LT
Tel: 0171 387 9692

Network 81/Action 81
1–7 Woodfield Terrace
Chapel Hill
Stansted
Essex CM24 8AJ
Tel: 01279 647415

Parents in Partnership
Unit 2 Ground Floor
70 South Lambeth Road
London SW8 1RL
Tel: 0171 735 7733

Voluntary organisations and agencies for specific SEN

You should be able to offer a list of voluntary agencies to parents so they may seek advice and information.

Association for all Speech Impaired Children (AFASIC)
347 Central Market
Smithfield
London EC1A 9NH

Association for Spina Bifida and Hydrocephalus (ASBAH)
ASBAH House
42 Park Road
Peterborough
PE1 2UQ
Tel: 0173 355 5988

Asthma Society
300 Upper Street
London N1 2XV

Barnardos
Banner's Lane
Barkeringside
Ilford
Essex
Tel: 0181 550 8822

British Diabetic Association
10 Queen Anne Street
London W1M OBD

British Dyslexia Association
98 London Road
Reading
Berkshire RG1 9NH

British Epilepsy Association
Anstey House
40 Hanover Square
Leeds LS1 BE

Coeliac Society
PO Box 220
High Wycombe
Bucks HP11 2HY

Cystic Fibrosis Research Trust
Alexandra House
5 Blythe Road
Bromley
Kent BR1 3RS

Down's Syndrome Association
153–5 Mitcham Road
London SW17 9BG

Dyslexic Institute
133 Gresham Road
Staines
Middlesex TW18 2AJ

Foundation for Conductive Education
6th Floor Clathorpe House
30 Hagley Road
Edgbaston
Birmingham M16 8QY

Hyperactive Children's Support Group
59 Meadowside
Angmering
Littlehampton
West Sussex BN16 4BW

Invalid Children's Aid-Nationwide ICAN
Barbican City Gate
1–3 Dufferin Street
London EC1Y 8NA

MENCAP
123 Golden Lane
London EX1Y ORT

MIND
Granta House
15–29 Broadway
London E15 4BQ

Muscular Dystrophy Group
7–11 Prescott Place
London SW4 6BS
Tel: 0171 720 8055

National Autistic Society
276 Willesden Lane
London NW2 5RB

National Eczema Society
Tavistock House North
Tavistock Square
London WC1H 9SE

Royal National Institute for the Blind
224 Great Portland Street
London W1N 6AA

Royal National Institute for the Deaf
105 Gower Street
London WC1E 6AH

SCOPE (formally Spastics Society)
16 Fitzroy Square
London W1P 5HQ

SENSE (National Deaf/Blind and Rubella Association)
11–13 Clifton Terrace
Finsbury Park
London N43 SR

Sickle Cell Society
Green Lodge
Barratts Green Road
London NW1D 7AP

SKILL
(National Bureau for Handicapped Students)
336 Brixton Road
London SW9 7AA

It is useful to build up a list of local support organisations. Several of the above may have local branches. Your LEA, Social Services Department, Citizens' Advice Bureau or Library Services can usually supply you with addresses.

A SENCO's guide to using the Internet

One of the features of the role of the SENCO is that a new challenge is usually just round the corner. To meet these challenges there is nothing more important than readily available up-to-date information and/or advice. Provided you have a reasonably fast computer attached to the Internet you should never have to move further than to your keyboard to obtain this.

First and foremost in the UK is the SENCO-FORUM. This is an open mail-list for all those involved in SEN work. A mail-list is a set of e-mail addresses held by the 'mailbase'. You enter your name on a list by 'subscribing' to the list. There is no subscription charge. Once you are a member of the list all messages that are sent to it arrive in your computer's mailbox. These may be cries for help, answers to such cries, comments on matters of current interest, criticism of previous contributions, or even criticism of the number of messages being sent to the list! Like the Internet itself a mail-list is an example of barely controlled anarchy. The 'listowner' will impose some sort of rule structure and normal 'netiquette' applies in that contributions should be kept short and to the point and advertising is sent to the listowner first. The main skill one needs is the ability to make judicious use of the 'delete' button. However, having said all that there is no doubt that SENCO-FORUM is a major source of help for a SENCO. As well as the day-to-day messages that stop you feeling isolated, there is an archive of previous messages which one can search.

Here you will find not only direct information but also suggestions for where further information can be found on the Internet. This is one of the main strengths of networking — each website you visit will pass you on to other sites dealing with similar areas of interest.

Below you will find a selection of websites that we have found useful, with brief notes showing what you may expect to find there. We do not pretend that they are the best or that the list is comprehensive only that you will find them a good starting point for the compilation of your own list of 'bookmarks' tailored to your own situation. If you get the answer that the site does not exist then try again deleting the last set of letters or numbers before the 'backslash' (/) until you get a 'hit'. The result will usually be a menu that allows you to move through the pages of the site.

To join SENCO-FORUM, send an e-mail message with no 'subject' to:
mailbase@mailbase.ac.uk
containing, in the body of the message, the command:
join senco-forum (your name)
(e.g. join senco-forum Fred Bloggs)

You must supply at least two words as a name, so for example F. Bloggs would be rejected (because there are no spaces and it is interpreted as a single word), but Fred Bloggs would be fine.

If you have a signature automatically added to your e-mails, follow the *join* command with a second line containing just the word *stop*. This will ensure that the mailbase software does not try (unsuccessfully) to interpret your signature as a command.

Possibly useful websites

The websites associated with the SENCO-FORUM

On the one you will find messages by dates, on the other they have been arranged by subject.

http://www.mailbase.ac.uk/lists/senco-forum/files/
Senco-FORUM Mailing List

http://www.mailbase.ac.uk/lists/senco-forum/archive.html
Message archive for SENCO-FORUM

Government sites

http://www.open.gov.uk/dfee/sen/senhome.htm The DfEE's
Special Educational Needs Division

http://www.dfee.gov.uk/ Welcome to DfEE

http://www.teach-tta.gov.uk./sentrain.htm Teacher Training
Agency

http://www.ngfl.gov.uk/ National Grid for Learning Home Page

http://www.coi.gov.uk/coi/depts/ Central Office of Information
Website

http://www.worldserver.pipex.com/coi/ Central Office of
Information

General SEN sites

Three sources of research information. The SCRE site is
particularly useful as you can 'download' factsheets and other
useful articles.

http://www.ed.ac.uk/~webscre/ Scottish Council for Research
in Education

http://www.nfer.ac.uk/ National Foundation for Educational
Research

http://www.scre.ac.uk/eera/ European Educational Research
Association (EERA)

This next site is probably your best jumping off point. It has
links to many excellent sources of data.

http://www.cant.ac.uk/xplanatory/xplan.htm Special Needs
Explanatory: Menu

A good example of how a list manager can help you keep up with a full range of views on a topic of major importance.

http://www.ncet.org.uk/senco/sources/debate.html Electronic debate on the Green Paper on Special Educational Needs

http://www.european-agency.com/ European Agency for Development in Special Needs Education

http://www.ncet.org.uk/senco/sources/senorgs.html Information Providers — special needs

http://www.fln.vcu.edu/ld/ld.html The Instant Access Treasure Chest

Examples of specialised sites

http://www.users.globalnet.co.uk/~ebdstudy/index.htm Disruptive and Disaffected Pupils in Mainstream Schools Index

http://www.bda-dyslexia.org.uk/ The British Dyslexia Association

http://www.interdys.org/ International Dyslexia Association

http://library.advanced.org/11799/data/dyspraxia.html Dyspraxia

http://www.tecquip.co.uk/needread.htm Need to Read Initiative

http://www.mailbase.ac.uk/lists/high-ability/files/boys.html NACE: National Association for Able Children in Education

http://www.rmplc.co.uk/eduweb/sites/accent/index.html ACE: Centre for IT information for pupils with a disability

Surfing the net

Most areas of disability now have websites and you can 'search the net' for information on most aspects of SEN.

Recommended competencies for Special Education Needs Coordinators (SENCO)

(As described in SENTC (1996) *Professional Development for SEN.*)

Coordinators for SEN in Mainstream School should be able to:

Context
- demonstrate their knowledge and understanding of relevant legislation and the Code of Practice for SEN
- show sensitivity to the needs of pupils with SEN and to their families
- draw upon knowledge and understanding of a wide range of SEN including factors within and outside schools which affect the social, physical, cognitive, emotional and behavioural development of pupils
- establish criteria for evaluating the 'successful learning' of pupils experiencing difficulties in learning
- special educational needs within a policy of equal opportunities

Curriculum
- identify and assess pupils' special educational needs and offer advice and support to colleagues in accordance with the Code of Practice
- use and evaluate a range of procedures and methods for assessing pupils' SEN
- develop, implement and evaluate a range of teaching strategies for meeting SEN

- design, write, support and monitor the implementation of Individual Education Plans as recommended in the Code of Practice
- develop and implement systems for recording, monitoring and reviewing the progress of pupils with SEN
- recognise and build on individual learning styles in order to teach effectively
- evaluate and make recommendations about the appropriate use to be made of various types of provision for pupils with SEN (Including placement in units and special classes or special schools)
- ensure that pupils with SEN have access to their curriculum entitlement
- make provision for pupils with SEN in relation to the statutory curriculum requirements and regulations including assessment within the National Curriculum
- demonstrate ability in basic literacy and numeracy teaching and teaching of study skills

Management
- facilitate the development, evaluation and review of school policies for SEN
- devise, implement and review school systems for identifying, assessing and reviewing pupils' SEN in accordance with the Code of Practice
- work in partnership with parents/carers
- work cooperatively in a consultancy capacity with teachers and other professionals
- plan, coordinate and manage different levels of meetings and case conferences
- work as a member of a multi-professional team
- advise and support colleagues on teaching and learning policies to meet diversity of needs
- advise and support colleagues about prevention and intervention strategies to be used with pupils experiencing:
  a) learning difficulties
  b) emotional and behavioural difficulties
- coordinate and review the work of teachers, special support assistants and support services personnel involved in meeting SEN
- play a major role in the professional development of ITT students and newly qualified teachers in order to enable

them to meet their responsibilities under the Code
of Practice

- help colleagues to identify their professional development
  needs in relation to meeting SEN and advise them
  accordingly, including planning and organising related
  school-based professional development activities
- manage and advise on appropriate resources and materials
- demonstrate good interpersonal and communication skills
  in every aspect of the roles described above.

SENCOs must be able to reflect on their own teaching and
behaviour in ways which enable them not only to be more
effective SEN coordinators with greater insights into their
responsibilities, but will enable them to enhance colleagues'
professional development in meeting individual educational
needs.

This list was the result of extensive consultation with SENCOs,
headteachers and other professionals supporting mainstream
schools. It was compiled by: Judith Jones, Lyndsay Peer, Mike
Johnson and Sylvia Phillips for the SENTC publication 1996
Professional Development for SEN.

References

ADAIR, J. (1983) *Effective Leadership.* London: Pan.

AYERS, H., CLARKE, D., ROSS, A. and BONATHAN, M. (1996) *Assessing Individual Needs: A Practical Approach*, (2nd edn), London: David Fulton.

BASTIANI, J. (1978) *Written Communication Between Home and School: A Report.* Nottingham: University of Nottingham.

BELBIN, R.M. (1981) *Management Teams: Why They Succeed or Fail*, Oxford: Herriemann.

BENNETT, N. (1995) *Managing Professional Teachers*, London: Paul Chapman.

BLACK, P. (1997) *Testing: Friend or Foe? Theory and Practice of Assessment and Testing*, London: Falmer Press.

BLAMIRES, M., ROBERTSON, C. and BLAMIRES, J. (1997) *Parent-Teacher Partnership: Practical Approaches to Meet Special Educational Needs*, London: Fulton.

BLANCHARD, K., CAREW, D. and PARISI-CAREW, E. (1994) *The One Minute Manager Builds High Performance Teams*, London: Harper Collins.

BOWERS, T. (1996) 'Special educational needs co-ordinators: Elements of the job in light of the Code of Practice', *Int. J. of Ed. Man.*, **10**, 5, pp. 27–31.

BRENNAN, W. (1985) *Curriculum for special needs*, Milton Keynes: Open University Press.

CHALLEN, M. and MAJORS, K. (1997) *Learning to Support: A Training Course for Special Support Assistants*, Bristol: Lucky Duck Publishing.

DAVIE, R. (1993) 'Interdisciplinary perspectives on assessment', in WOLFENDALE, S. (ed.) *Assessing Special Educational Needs*, London: Cassell pp. 134–149.

DEAN, J. (1987) *Managing the Primary School*, London: Croome Helm.

DES (1978) *Special Educational Needs: Report the Committee of Enquiry into the Education of Handicapped Children and Young People*, (The Warnock Report), London: HMSO.

DES (1989) *Discipline in Schools* (The Elton Report), London: HMSO.

DFE (1994) *Code of Practice on the Identification and Assessment of Special Educational Needs*, London: HMSO.

DfEE (1997a) *The SENCO Guide*, London: HMSO.

DfEE (1997b) *Excellence for All Children*, (Green Paper), London: HMSO.

DfEE (1997c) *SEN Tribunals: How to Appeal*, London: HMSO.

DUNHAM, J. (1992) *Stress in Teaching*, (2nd edn), London: Routledge.

EVERARD, K.B. and MORRIS, G. (eds) (1996) *Effective School Management*, (3rd edn), London: Paul Chapman.

FOX, G. (1993) *Special Need and Assistants: Working in Partnership with Teachers*, London: David Fulton.

FULLAN, M. (1991) *The New Meaning of Educational Change*, (2nd edn), London: Cassell.

GALVIN, P., MERCER, S. and COSTA, P. (1991) *Building a Better-behaved School*, London: Longman.

GARNER, P. (1996) ' "Go forth and co-ordinate": What special needs co-ordinators think about the Code of Practice', *School Organisation*, **16**, 2, pp. 179–86.

GASCOIGNE, E. (1995) *Working with Parents as Partners in SEN*, London: David Fulton.

GIPPS, C. (1994) *Beyond Testing: Towards a Theory of Educational Assessment*, London: Falmer Press.

GROSS, J. (1996) *Special Educational Needs in the Primary School: A Practical Guide*, (2nd edn), Buckingham: Open University.

HART, S. (1986) 'Evaluating support teaching, *Gnosis*, September, pp. 25–31.

HINTON, S. (1993) 'Assessing for special needs and supporting learning in the early years and nursery education' in WOLFENDALE, S. (ed.) *Assessing Special Educational Needs*, London: Cassell, pp. 37–56.

HOBART, C. and FRANKEL, J. (1994) *A Practical Guide to Child Observation*, Cheltenham: Stanley Thornes (Publishers) Ltd.

HONEY, P. (1988) *Improve Your People Skills*, London: Institute of Personal Management.

HORNBY, G. (1995) *Working with Parents of Children with Special Needs*, London: Cassell.

HULL, J. (1994) *Assessment and Record-keeping for Special Educational needs in Mainstream Schools*, Stafford: NASEN.

LEIGH, A. (1988) *Effective Change: Twenty Ways to Make It Happen*, London: Institute of Personnel Management.

LEIGH, A. and MAYNARD, M. (1995) *Leading Your Team*, London: Nicholas Brealey.

LEWIS, A., NEILL, S.R. and CAMPBELL, R. (1996) *The Implementation of the Code of Practice in Primary and Secondary Schools*, Coventry: Institute of Education, University of Warwick.

LINDSAY, G. (1981) *The Infant Rating Scale*, Sevenoaks: Hodder & Stoughton.

LLOYD-JONES, R. (1985) *How to Produce Better Worksheets*, London: Hutchinson.

MACINTOSH, H.G. and HALE, D.E. (1976) *Assessment and the Secondary School Teacher*, London: Routledge and Kegan Paul.

MOSS, G. (1995) 'Managing teaching and non-teaching staff', *Special Children*, May, pp. M1–M7.

OFSTED (1996) *The implementation of the Code of Practice for Pupils with Special Educational Needs*, London: HMSO.

PANTER, S. (1996) *How to Survive as a SEN Co-ordinator*, Lichfield: QED.

PEARSON, L. and QUINN, J. (1986) *The Bury Infant Checklist*, Windsor: NFER-Nelson.

PHILLIPS, S. and COCKETT, P. (1995) *SEN: Putting the Code to Work (Primary)*, London: Pitman.

PLANT, R. (1987) *Managing Change and Making it Stick*, London: Fontana.

POSTLETHWAITE, K. and HACKNEY, A. (1988) *Provision for Pupils with Special Needs in Mainstream Schools*, London: MacMillan.

PUMFREY, D. (1991) *Improving Children's Reading in the Junior School: Challenges and Responses*, London: Cassell.

SENTC (1996) *Professional Development for SEN*, Stafford: SEN Training Consortium.

SHARMA, M. (1990) Lecture to teachers in Tameside LEA.

SMITH, C.J. (1982) 'Helping colleagues cope — consultant role for the remedial teacher', *Remedial Education*, **17**, 1 pp 75–78.

STANSFIELD, J. (1996) 'Lightening the Load', *Special Children*, January, pp 23–25.

Teacher Training Agency (TTA) (1998) *National Standards for Special Educational Needs Co-ordinators*, London: TTA.

THOMAS, G. (1985) 'Room Management in Mainstream Education', *Ed. Res.*, **27**, 3, pp. 186–93.

TRETHOWAN, D. (1989) *Communication: Management in Education*, London: Industrial Society Press.

TROPMAN, J.E. (1996) *Effective Meetings*, San Francisco: Sage Publications.

WESTWOOD, P. (1997) *Commonsense Methods for Children with Special Needs*, (3rd edn), London: Routledge.

WHITAKER, P. (1993) *Managing Change in Schools*, Buckingham: Open University

WHITAKER, P. (1994) *Practical Communication Skills in Schools*, Harlow: Longman.

WIDLAKE, P. (ed.) (1996) *The Good Practice Guide to Special Educational Needs*, Birmingham: Questions Publishing.

WOLFENDALE, S. (1992) *Primary Schools and Special Needs*, London: Cassell.

WOLFENDALE, S. (ed.) (1997) *Working with Parents of SEN Children after the Code of Practice*, London: David Fulton.

Index

ORDER FORM

Post: *Customer Services Department, Falmer Press, Rankine Road, Basingstoke, Hampshire, RG24 8PR*
Tel: *(01256) 813000* **Fax**: *(01256) 479438*
E-mail: *book.orders@tandf.co.uk*

10% DISCOUNT AND FREE P&P FOR SCHOOLS OR INDIVIDUALS ORDERING THE COMPLETE SET
ORDER YOUR SET NOW. WITH CREDIT CARD PAYMENTS, YOU WON'T BE CHARGED TILL DESPATCH.

TITLE	DUE	ISBN	PRICE	QTY
SUBJECT LEADERS' HANDBOOKS SET		**(RRP £207.20)**	**£185.00**	
Coordinating Science	2/98	0 7507 0688 0	£12.95	
Coordinating Design and Technology	2/98	0 7507 0689 9	£12.95	
Coordinating Maths	2/98	0 7507 0687 2	£12.95	
Coordinating Physical Education	2/98	0 7507 0693 7	£12.95	
Coordinating History	2/98	0 7507 0691 0	£12.95	
Coordinating Music	2/98	0 7507 0694 5	£12.95	
Coordinating Geography	2/98	0 7507 0692 9	£12.95	
Coordinating English at Key Stage 1	4/98	0 7507 0685 6	£12.95	
Coordinating English at Key Stage 2	4/98	0 7507 0686 4	£12.95	
Coordinating IT	4/98	0 7507 0690 2	£12.95	
Coordinating Art	4/98	0 7507 0695 3	£12.95	
Coordinating Religious Education	Late 98	0 7507 0613 9	£12.95	
Management Skills for SEN Coordinators	Late 98	0 7507 0697 X	£12.95	
Building a Whole School Assessment Policy	Late 98	0 7507 0698 8	£12.95	
Curriculum Coordinator and OFSTED Inspection	Late 98	0 7507 0699 6	£12.95	
Coordinating Curriculum in Smaller Primary School	Late 98	0 7507 0700 3	£12.95	

Value of Books	
P&P*	
Total	

I wish to pay by:

*Please add p&p
orders up to £25   *10%*
orders from £25 to £50   *5%*
orders over £50   *free*

❑ Cheque (*Pay* Falmer Press)
❑ Pro-forma invoice
❑ Credit Card (*Mastercard / Visa / AmEx*)

Card Number _____ *Expiry Date* _____
Signature _____
Name _____ *Title/Position* _____
School _____
Address _____
_____
Postcode _____ *Country* _____
Tel no. _____ *Fax* _____
E-mail _____

☐ If you do not wish to receive further promotional information from the Taylor&Francis Group, please tick box.
All prices are correct at time of going to print but may change without notice

Ref: 1197BFSLAD